Leadership
in
Constant Change
embracing a new missional reality

TERRY R. HAMRICK

© 2015

Published in the United States by Nurturing Faith Inc., Macon GA,
www.nurturingfaith.net.

Library of Congress Cataloging-in-Publication Data is available.

ISBN: 978-1-938514-72-2

All rights reserved. Printed in the United States of America through a partnership of
Nurturing Faith and the Cooperative Baptist Fellowship.

New Revised Standard Version Bible, ©1989, Division of Christian Education of the
National Council of the Churches of Christ in the United States of America and are
used by permission. All rights reserved.

Cooperative Baptist Fellowship
160 Clairemont Avenue
Suite 500
Decatur, GA 30030
www.cbf.net
800.352.8741

CONTENTS

Foreword v

Introduction 1

Part 1: Transition in a New Context 5

    Chapter 1: Who Moved My World? 7

    Chapter 2: The Missional Journey 15

    Chapter 3: Leading in Constant Change 31

    Chapter 4: Qualities of Missional Leaders 45

Part 2: Applications and Resources for a Missional Reality . 63

    Chapter 5: Changing Role in the Community 65

    Chapter 6: From Missions Toward Missional 75

    Chapter 7: What Does a Leader Look Like? 91

    Bibliography 105

    Appendix: Sermons by Jack Glasgow 107

FOREWORD

There is no harder job on the planet than leading a local congregation in today's world! Every day is filled with challenges beyond expectations. Every day is filled with criticism and second guessing from those who don't appreciate the work. Every day is filled with the impact of change, of social media, and of instant connectivity. The constant barrage of change management leaves little time for spiritual contemplation, prayer, and strategic thought.

Into this culture and climate of change and criticism comes a word of hope and help. Terry Hamrick, former coordinator for missional leadership at the Cooperative Baptist Fellowship and career congregational educator, brings insights that can assist congregational leaders. Hamrick writes with an insight that comes from his continual study and examination of congregational leaders. He understands congregational systems and he empathizes with congregational leaders. His words are definitely for such a time as this! This is the second edition of this work. The first edition sold out quickly to denominational leaders, seminary professors, and pastoral leaders across our landscape.

Through a series of case studies, Hamrick brings real life examples to this work. Congregations are facing issues that they have never dealt with before. Congregational leaders are being asked to lead through issues for which they are not adequately equipped. Anxieties are running high both in pastor, staff ministers, lay leaders, and congregants. Everyone is hoping for, praying for a "magic" solution that doesn't exist. Hamrick addresses the state of the church today, the challenges for leaders today, and offers hope for a continued vitality and vibrancy of the local congregation.

A recent interview among business leaders drew several conclusions:

- The only thing constant is change.
- Everything is at crisis mode and leaders now have to be in constant response mode.
- We are a technological society; every organization is a "tech" organization.
- The missional response is not programmable or predictable.
- The missional response is contextual, organic, and dynamic for each congregation.
- Nothing never happens.

Drawing upon some of the best in scholarly research and his own experiences, Hamrick brings the reader into proactive responses and hopeful dialogue. He states the fundamental challenge quite clearly, "How do we be the people of God in the midst of such transition?" And he gives insights that lead to practical applications not predictable prescriptions.

Ultimately, the responsibility for leading is upon the leadership team. Yet, leadership does not have to be done in isolation or without good counsel. Hamrick has provided good insights and good counsel through a rich interweaving of good thinkers and good practitioners.

Along the way you'll have opportunities to stop and reflect on your context and apply these thoughts to where you serve. Also included in this work are a series of sermons from Jack Glasgow, pastor of Zebulon Baptist Church in Zebulon, NC. Jack brings the thoughts on leadership into wonderful sermonic insight and challenge that further brings application.

This is a wonderful tool to help pastors and other congregational leaders. I'm proud to have been part of the idea germination and the creative formation. I'm honored to call Dr. Hamrick friend and colleague. And, I'm extremely pleased to offer this to you for your ministry and work.

Bo Prosser, Ed. D.
Cooperative Baptist Fellowship

INTRODUCTION

Welcome to First Church. The Advent banners are being hung. Choirs are rehearsing overtime, and all are anticipating a great December. In spite of all the activity and preparation, concerns are never far away. Yes, the Advent schedule is the same, but many other things have changed. The ushers no longer have to stand ready to place folding chairs in the aisles to accommodate the December crowds. The pastor is no longer invited to offer a Christmas message at the local high school. The music minister can no longer rely on church members to fill the orchestra.

Things are different. The people seem more anxious. The conversations in committee meetings have also changed. The finance committee used to meet to discuss how to disburse the budget overage. Now they are more likely to be talking about how much they have to reduce the missions giving or staff salaries in order to pay the bills. The missions committee's primary concern in December once was enlisting enough volunteers to deliver Christmas baskets to the needy. Now the challenge is rationing the limited supply among so many needy persons.

The leaders of First Church were born into a world that no longer exists. The tried-and-true models for doing church are becoming more tired than true. The spirit of abundance has given over to a pervasive sense of scarcity. People can enjoy many appealing and competing activities on Sunday other than attending church. Pastors are under increasing pressure to bring the church, and its members, back to the status it enjoyed in an earlier day. Lay leaders and ministry budgets are under increasing pressure to maintain the various programs and functions of the church.

Some folk suggest singing choruses or other works not found in the hymnal during worship. What's wrong with these people? Where did they come from? Don't they understand how we do things at First Church?

While some details may vary, this same story is being played out in congregations across the country. Congregations face some critical decisions. Things are not working. What are they going to do? Are they going to expend their energy trying to maintain the familiar, or are they going to try to figure out how to embrace the world in which they find themselves?

Congregations no longer have the income to do all the things they have always done. Hard choices are required. Mission and ministry budgets are being reduced, often on a quarterly basis. Beloved ministers are having their compensation reduced and sometimes even having their positions eliminated. Active lay leaders are being pressed to move to another church because they want their children to have fully functioning programs. The signs of stress are all around.

An all-too-typical response to this transitional crisis is to ask: "What's wrong with the people who should be participating in our congregation? Why don't they join us? What's *their* problem?" Over time the questions can turn inward: "What's wrong with us? What's *our* problem?" While neither set of questions has a simple answer, such questions tend to raise the level of anxiety within the congregation and can lead to some unhealthy responses.

Often anxious congregations are drawn into the trap of claiming simple solutions to fix complex problems. "We need to change our worship style." "We need to hire a public relations consultant." "We need to relocate to a better part of town." "Our folks need to be more committed and give more." And all too often, "We need a different pastor, one that has the answers we want to hear."

Are we asking the right questions? More and more congregations have realized that these questions and the resulting answers do not solve their problems. While some or all of these actions may eventually be necessary, they are an inadequate starting place for the challenges congregations are facing today.

This book has been written for these congregations and their leaders. In the chapters that follow, I invite you to join me as we search for the questions our congregations should be asking and together explore some possible answers.

This work is organized into two parts. Part 1 focuses on the new context churches find themselves in today and some key resources to aid in their transition to this new place. Chapter 1 describes the context of congregations in constant change and the situation their leaders find themselves in and suggests a missional perspective that invites the church to be the church in this new reality.

After we recognize and embrace our context, chapter 2 invites us to explore this missional perspective that places primary focus on God's mission rather than the church's mission. In this chapter we will explore theological, missiological, and ecclesiastical support for the missional perspective.

In chapter 3 the focus shifts to the task of transition and the challenge of leading transitions in a congregation. Two different resources will be offered as potential guides for this journey, the work on transitions by William Bridges and adaptive leadership theory offered by Ronald Heifietz et al.

The final chapter in part 1 discusses five specific leadership qualities that have emerged as being helpful in leading transition in a congregation.

Part 2 attempts to take the issues and resources discussed in part 1 and apply them to a congregational setting. First Church, fictional yet representative, will be used to illustrate how we might apply these resources to our own congregations.

Chapter 5 focuses on the implications of a changed relationship between First Church and its surrounding community and the wider world. Particular attention is given to identifying "endings" First Church is experiencing.

In chapter 6 we see some of the challenges First Church faces as it begins the transition process from an institutional to a missional perspective.

The final chapter brings us back to focus on the leader. Through dealing with some real issues we see how congregational leaders can become adaptive leaders and express the qualities of missional leadership.

A series of sermons and discussion guides has been included in an appendix. Pastor Jack Glasgow prepared and delivered these sermons and led the discussions that followed. Many thanks to Jack for his insights and his generous spirit.

PART 1

Transition in a New Context

CHAPTER 1

Who Moved My World?

As we approached the end of the millennium and change was all around us, the subject of transition gained increasing popularity. Now, more than a decade into the new century, the subject of transition has moved from a novel idea to a survival strategy. Churches of every kind are facing unprecedented challenges. Attendance, giving, and loyalty to the institution are decreasing. The long-assumed prominence of the church in the community is no longer holding. Relevance is being questioned, and leadership is under increasing pressure to turn things around.

We are experiencing more than just a change in centuries; the reality is that we are dealing with an epochal shift in our existence. The late Peter Drucker, hardly an alarmist, describes our situation with his usual clarity: "Every few hundred years in Western history there occurs a sharp transformation. Within a few short decades, society rearranges itself—its worldview; its basic values; its social and political structure; its arts; its key institutions. Fifty years later, there is a new world. And the people born then cannot even imagine the world in which their grandparents lived and into which their own parents were born. We are currently living through just such a transformation" (Drucker, 1993).

If Ducker is correct, we are just beginning to experience this transition. How does the church respond when our culture rearranges its basic values? What are the implications for the church when social and political structures are reordered? How does a congregation accommodate an unprecedented range of diverse perspectives?

Pollster Daniel Yankelovich made a statement 30 years ago that should get our attention. Like Drucker he observed that our culture is in the midst of "a hinge of history" that began in approximately 1950 and will not conclude until 100 years later around 2050. When I first ran across this observation, I was energized. I was young, and I had little investment in all the institutions in the direct path of this change. Then I had a second reaction. I was born in 1950; so if Yankelovich is correct, then my entire life would be spent in this period of radical reorientation. My entire ministry would be spent working with congregations and individuals who, at best, are looking back longingly to a more certain time. They would struggle mightily to find relevance in their present world and in the world to come. That has proven to be so.

Phyllis Tickle, in *The Great Emergence*, suggests that such a time of transition is nothing new for the church. Her premise is that the church has experienced profound transitions in its relationship with culture, again echoing Drucker, roughly every 500 years. According to Tickle, the mega-transition we are currently experiencing, which she has named "The Great Emergence," is just the latest such period.

If these folk are correct, then church leaders have no place to hide. The huge tidal wave of change will wash over everything: our world, our cultures, our institutions, our values, and our relationships. Both individuals and systems seem to have a built-in response mechanism that tries to minimize and contain change and its resultant anxiety. If a system can minimize the change, it will be easier to manage. Systems, whether cultures or individuals, resist change in favor of homeostasis. We want to be able to rely on reality as we understand it and have experienced it in order to stay "normal."

Congregations have honed this skill into a fine art. Many lifelong church members struggle with transition and change affecting every aspect of their lives, but they almost desperately want their church to stay the same. Our churches are filled with competing views of what it should look like. I have been in hundreds of churches over the years and have observed with great sadness that for many, if the year 1955 ever comes back, they will be ready!

Daniel Aleshire, executive director of the Association of Theological Schools, describes the church's dilemma. He observed that in the 1950s and 1960s the church was busily going about its work, and the culture was in the background cheering it on. Sundays were sacred times, and nothing secular would be scheduled. In the South, at least, even Wednesday evenings were off-limits to all but church activities. The communities in which the churches found themselves were fairly homogeneous.

Aleshire noted that some time ago the culture stopped cheering the church on and starting competing. The church, however, continued to act as if it were still in sync with its surroundings. Church has now become one of several options on Sunday. Communities, more often than not, include a variety of ethnic, cultural, racial, and religious groups. Welcome to the world of constant change. It is not a matter of staying "normal." Constant change is the new reality.

Many historians, scholars, and cultural observers have declared that we are experiencing the final gasps of Christendom. Christianity became the recognized and favored religion of the Roman Empire when Emperor Constantine reunited the empire in 324 CE. The Christian movement had moved from a persecuted sect to the established church of the empire. For more than a thousand years the church and culture shared a symbiotic relationship that we have come to call Christendom.

Some historians argue that the seeds for the ending of Christendom were planted in the soil of the Renaissance and the

Reformation in the fifteenth and sixteenth centuries. We are just now harvesting the mature fruit of this slow and deliberate process.

Reading over these last paragraphs, a tangible illustration of the end of Christendom jumps out. We have changed how we designate years from Christendom's BC (Before Christ) and AD (Anno Domini) to the post-Christendom BCE (Before the Common Era) and CE (Common Era).

Change is everywhere, washing over us. The question we are being called to consider is not: How do we avoid or minimize the effect of change? The fundamental question is clear: What does it mean to be the people of God in the midst of great transition?

Pause for a moment and picture what this transition looks like in your context. What changes are having the most impact on you and your congregation? How are you responding to constant change in our world?

In a lecture at Southwestern Baptist Theological Seminary in March 1993, Leonard Sweet was the first person I heard use the "tidal wave" metaphor to help us understand what is happening. He extended that metaphor in books that followed: *SoulTsunami* and *Aqua Church*. Sweet made clear that the tidal wave was coming and that it was going to wash over all of us. He also suggests three possible responses we can make in reaction to this tidal wave of change.

First, we can deny that any change is happening and continue to function as usual. Churches continue to operate as they always have and hope somehow things will get better. They find the complexity of the changes facing them too much to handle. Their flight response kicks in when faced with increasing ambiguity. Our country is full of such churches. Their participation has been on steady decline for years, and the faithful fewer and fewer keep trying to do church. Loyalty and perseverance are admirable character traits, but going through the motions and holding on is not what church is about.

A second response to this tidal wave of change is to retreat into our bunker and preserve our ways until the wave passes. This approach acknowledges the tidal wave of change but is determined not to be corrupted by it. The resurgence of fundamentalism across many faith groups provides one illustration of this response. This protectionist posture can isolate the gospel from a world that so desperately needs to hear good news.

Modernity gave us many good and meaningful things. Two interrelated developments in particular have had a significant impact on life in America in general and congregational life in particular—the Industrial Revolution and the scientific method. We will discuss production and the assembly line later. In a turn pregnant with irony, the domain of science, so often rejected by fundamentalism, has contributed to its flowering.

Scientific research methodology is most often based on finding the one correct answer to a problem. Beginning in modernity and continuing to the present day, we have been on a pursuit of the right answer for each problem whether simple or complex. For fundamentalists, regardless of their faith traditions, the goals are to have the right answers and to protect and defend those answers. We learn in elementary physics that nature abhors a vacuum.

Sweet suggests that the approach we can take is to hoist our sail and see where God's Spirit takes us. As the winds of change blow across God's creation, we are being called to put ourselves in a position to hear and respond to God's leading. This response calls us to an awkward place of vulnerability as leaders and institutions. These are not qualities highly valued in leaders today.

If we are honest with ourselves, we find something compelling in each of these responses. Many of us long for the familiar. We want to protect what we have and keep it safe for as long as we need it. And yes, we too, want to be a part of God's great adventure. These three responses have a key difference, however. The first two responses are natural. They are fairly easy to do, and we will have no trouble finding others willing to join us. These responses require little leadership and discernment. The third response is a different matter. This response is not so easy. This response really is outside our comfort zone. This response to the constant change requires spiritually insightful leadership and a community that understands and embraces its role in realizing God's mission.

Too many churches and their leaders are asking the wrong questions. Their actions, their priorities, and their heightened level of anxiety point to some fundamental questions: How do we stop, or at least ignore, the flow of history? Should our goal be to try to stop constant change or to learn to lead in the midst of it? How do we protect and preserve our way of being and doing church? Many churches are spending their energies trying to protect their traditions and hunker down and do what they know best while others are pretending that it is still 1955.

These are more often the "safe" responses to this time of great change. *Safe* here refers to the strategy that is least disruptive to the fellowship. Church after church has elevated peace and harmony within the congregation to its top operational priority. Churches do not want to risk anything that might sour their sweet fellowship.

There is nothing wrong with wanting a warm, caring fellowship. That is to be desired. Such a community is important as the congregation tries to connect with God's mission in the world. The problem comes when the quality of the fellowship as measured by the absence of conflict and disagreement becomes the church's primary concern. Conflict always appears in times of transition.

While we should not be surprised by this development, more appropriate questions should be guiding us in these times: What is God calling us to be and do at this unique place and time? What parts of our tradition, our familiar, can help us answer this question and inform our journey? What parts are interfering with our ability to hear God's call, and how can we know the difference?

These are some of the missional questions requiring a clear understanding of God's mission in the world. Congregational leaders find themselves in the shadows of these questions. Other questions naturally emerge. How do we put ourselves in a position to hear God's call? How do we honor our tradition and use it to propel us toward responding to God's call in the twenty-first century?

These questions call congregations today to embrace an unprecedented level of intentionality regarding their futures. Most of us were trained to minister and lead in a world that no longer exists. Many of the certainties we counted on are no longer certain. Many of our long-held views are coming under increasing pressure. Our perspectives on God, church, mission, community, and personal responsibility were formed in a Christendom culture. We find our most basic understandings being challenged in a post-Christendom context. When congregations and their leaders find themselves at this place, they may be ready to enter the missional conversation.

CHAPTER 2

The Missional Journey

The church is in the midst of an epochal shift, and it could not be better news! What? Are you crazy? How could such a transition, filled with disruption and uncertainty, possibly be good?

Just such a circumstance is inviting congregations around the world to embrace a new understanding of what it means to be the people of God in the world. Congregational systems, like most systems, seek and reward equilibrium. The difficulty comes when circumstances change, and new initiative is called for. Systemic pressure increases just to stay the course. The level of change the church is experiencing today is too great to ignore. Opportunities beckon us to discover new insights into what God is calling us to be and do.

The church has always had to live with the tension of being *in* the world and not *of* the world. Some would argue that at least in twentieth-century America the church found itself less *in* the world and more *of* the world.

The nineteenth century saw the beginnings of the Industrial Revolution that came into full flower in the first decades of the twentieth century. Success became more and more measured by wealth. Wealth was more and more understood as being tied to one's ability to produce. Assembly lines, large factories, and migrating workforces were focused on the bottom line. Workers were paid on what they were able to produce. I grew up in an area filled with textile mills. The language I heard was that folk "worked production." They were paid based on the number of spools of thread they wound or the yards of cloth they wove in an eight-hour shift. Our hope and worth were based on what we could produce.

This was the environment in which the church in America found itself. The church's worth and value were measured in large part by what it could produce. That bottom line influenced how churches understood their roles and relationships in the world. By assuming responsibility for mission, churches found a focus for their production efforts. A Christological missiology became predominant especially in evangelical congregations. The ecclesial focus became obedience to the Great Commission. The church had a measurable mission and purpose.

To accomplish this mission, churches needed a faithful membership that either participated in or supported those who participated in evangelism. This was a quantifiable task. The church's mission became its organizing principle. The congregational system adapted in amazing fashion and with relative speed. The local church, while never giving up on being community, began quickly to value programs and organization that helped it focus on the bottom line. Tension developed between the spiritual development of the individual believer and the health and growth of the organization. An assumption emerged over time that if it was good for the church, then it was good for the individual. The need for evaluation also aided this development. Measuring and evaluating a person's spiritual maturity is difficult, but measuring and evaluating attendance and offerings is easy. The church in many ways bought into the importance of a measurable bottom line.

The argument is not with the need to evaluate or for the church to have a vision. The problem develops when we focus on an inadequate bottom line that invites us to evaluate and give priority to lesser things. Many congregations today find themselves in a difficult place. Over the decades, almost imperceptibly, their measure for success became institutional metrics. Success was measured by attendance, giving, and relative harmony within the fellowship. Individuals have tacitly equated their vision with the growth and harmony of their congregations. That arrangement works as long as the congregation is growing and the fellowship is enjoying relative peace and harmony. However, when this is no longer the case, when what they depend on for vision is threatened, these folk get anxious. These evaluative measures were, in most cases, initially offered with the assumption that they represented conditions fostering spiritual growth and contributing to kingdom values. The church today finds itself in a different place.

The churches that formed me and several prior generations were filled with wonderful people doing many good things. We were taught, formed, trained, and called to serve. I loved the church and wanted it to succeed. I still do. The problem was not that we had good program organizations. The problem was our vision. We as church leaders bought into modernity—lock, stock, and barrel. Unintentionally and almost without notice our bottom line changed. As our programs became larger and more complex and our communities became more diverse, we shifted our measures. We began to focus on what was obvious. We equated the church's effectiveness with its production, which was primarily measured as participation in programs. We counted attendance. We counted dollars. We counted converts. We counted visitors. We counted prospects. We counted new members. We did everything possible to avoid conflict and disagreement because that could affect our production. The prophetic word often went unspoken because it did not make a positive contribution to our bottom line.

Some among us responded to the increased diversity by imposing increasingly narrow rules of acceptable belief. Our measure became right belief and practice. We taught our folk, both implicitly and explicitly, that being a good church member was the same thing as being a good participant in the kingdom of God. Taken to the extreme, we put God in our safe and manageable church box.

We limited God and the expression of God's mission to our measurable, logical, and orderly structures. We traded a kingdom view for a congregational view. When the church's mission is substituted for God's mission, many participating in God's kingdom limit their actions and attitudes to being good church members.

An ironic and sobering twist comes into play here. The church is to be a place where hopeless people come to find hope. Unfortunately, many congregations today are desperately looking for hope themselves. Pollsters and researchers offer grim predictions on the number of congregations that will close their doors in the next 20 years. Their predictions state that up to 50 percent of congregations existing today will no longer exist by 2050 (Barna, 2005). This is just one of the tangible evidences of the period of transition we are experiencing. Questions we must address include: What do current circumstances say about the church's vision? In what or whom do we find vision? Where do churches that are having difficulty meeting budgets find vision? Where do ministers facing an increasingly long list of harmony-threatening issues find vision? Where does our world, broken and bleeding, turn for vision? What does hope look like in the midst of an epochal transition and change?

The challenge for us from this point is to understand the call of God upon the church. What is God calling the church, and you and me, to be and do at this unique place and time? We need to locate a new bottom line, or lines, that will enable us as the people of God to call all of God's creation to focus on God's mission in the world. And we need to develop leaders, both clergy and laity, that are equipped to help us accomplish this mission. These are the most significant transitional challenges facing the church today.

So, where do the church and its leaders turn for vision in an increasingly hopeless time? The answer is simple, profound, and loaded with implications—to God and God's mission. Yes, even in the midst of our sophistication, our education, our industriousness, our connectedness, and our experience, we are confronted with the clear reality that we are not God!

We often think and act as if we are, but we are not. We come, you and I, needy and confused, just as generations before us have come, searching for hope, meaning, and purpose. Previous generations have placed their hope in a variety of things, only to be disappointed. We come, having placed our hope, at least in part, in the institutional church, only to be disappointed once again. We stand at the end of the first decade of the twenty-first century, being called to echo the ancients, "God is love," and "Jesus is Lord." We must return to this fundamental starting place for all Christ followers as we search for hope for our future. The mission is God's not the church's. The mission is God's not ours.

God's Mission, Our Vision

No group has been more helpful to me in articulating our current challenge than The Gospel in Our Culture Network (*www.gocn.org*). This group of academics and practitioners building on the work of Leslie Newbigin, David Bosch, and other theologians and missiologists have articulated the challenge. This group has invited us to a vision of what the church should be and do in the world in which we find ourselves. This collaborative effort is inviting the church to be *missional*. The church is at its best when it finds its hope, meaning, and purpose in engaging in God's mission in the world.

The concept of being *missional* has grown in popularity over the last few years. The missional perspective found some of its clearest focus in the book, *The Missional Church: A Vision for the Sending of the Church in North America* by Darrell Guder. The heart of this work can be summed up by this oft-quoted passage from the introduction: "The ecclesiocentric understanding of mission has been replaced during this century by a profoundly theocentric reconceptualization of Christian mission" (Guder, 1998). The missional conversation, then, is our response to this fundamental change in perspective from a church-centered mission to a God-centered mission.

Since the publication of Guder's book in 1998, the use of the term *missional* has exploded, with the danger that *missional* will become such a buzzword that the power of this perspective will be lost. The term *missional* is used to describe everything from life-reorienting experiences to budget campaigns. Partly to address this dilution of the concept, Craig Van Gelder and Dwight J. Zscheile have written a helpful book, *The Missional Church in Perspective: Mapping Trends and Shaping the Conversation*. Van Gelder and Zscheile have identified four themes that have emerged from the missional conversation to give us a framework for understanding this reconceptualization:

1. God is a missionary God who sends the church into the world. This understanding shifts the agency of mission from the church to God. It is God's mission that has a church rather than a church that has a mission.

2. God's mission in the world is related to the reign (kingdom) of God. This understanding makes the work of God in the world larger than the mission of the church, although the church is directly involved in the reign (kingdom) of God.

3. The missional church is an incarnational (versus an attractional) ministry sent to engage a postmodern, post-Christendom, globalized context. This understanding requires every congregation to take on a missionary posture for engaging its local context, with this missionary engagement shaping everything a congregation does.

4. The internal life of the missional church focuses on every believer living as a disciple engaging in mission. This understanding makes every member a minister,

with the spiritual growth of every disciple becoming the primary focus as the body is built up to participate more fully in God's mission in the world (Van Gelder and Zscheile, 2011).

A closer look at these four themes should help us get a clearer picture of some of the power and potential of being missional.

Missionary God

It is easy to pronounce that we are about God's mission. But what does that mean? We must proceed with caution here. God's mission needs to be defined and articulated, but we must be careful not to let our individual perspectives skew the definition. Sadly, we can each recount stories where selfish interests were justified as being central to God's mission.

David Bosch in *Transforming Mission* defines God's mission as follows: "Missio Dei (God's mission) is God's self-revelation as the One who loves the world, God's involvement in and with the world, the nature and activity of God, which embraces both the church and the world, and in which the church is privileged to participate. Missio Dei enunciates the good news that God is a God-for-people" (Bosch, 1991).

Here is a new bottom line for the church. "God is a God-for-people." The focus here is God and God's relationship with creation and more particularly humankind. Bosch did not say that God is a God for churches. The church is not the focus of God's mission but an instrument for its accomplishment. This is where we begin to discover our source of hope, meaning, and purpose.

Guder clarifies, "But it has taken us decades to realize that mission is not just a program of the church. It defines the church as God's sent people. Either we are defined by mission, or we reduce the scope of the gospel and the mandate of the church. Thus our challenge is to move from church with mission to missional church" (Guder, 1998).

The dominant Christendom mission/church division is being challenged by a Trinitarian missiology. God is a missionary God. God the Father sent the Son. The Father and the Son sent (and send) the Spirit. All three send the church and individuals to be about God's mission in the world.

Reign of God

The reign or kingdom of God was a key theme of Jesus. He proclaimed that the kingdom has come near. He identified it as his purpose: "But he said to them, 'I must proclaim the good news of the kingdom of God to the other cities also; for I was sent for this purpose'" (Luke 4:43).

Jesus used kingdom imager when he taught: "The kingdom of heaven may be compared to someone who sowed good seed in his field." And he gave this instruction to his disciples as he sent them out: "As you go, proclaim the good news, 'The kingdom of heaven has come near'" (Matt. 10:7).

The natural question, particularly for the Western mind, is, What does the reign of God look like? George Hunsberger points us to philosopher Arthur Holmes who describes this reign as *shalom*. "It envisions a world characterized by peace, justice and celebration" (Guder, 1998).

Paul, while addressing disagreements over dietary laws, offers this view. "For the kingdom of God is not food and drink but righteousness and peace and joy in the Holy Spirit" (Rom. 14:17).

Hunsberger warns that often he hears language like "building the kingdom" or "extending the kingdom," while the New Testament uses words like "receive" and "enter." "The reign of God is first of all a gift one receives" (Guder, 1998). Second, "The reign of God is a realm—a space, an arena, a zone—that may be inhabited" (Guder, 1998).

The kingdom of heaven is a gift, and it is a place to be experienced. As we follow Jesus' invitation to follow him, we are being called to live into this space. We are called both to experience and contribute to peace, justice, and celebration. *The kingdom has come near* should be a source of great hope for all.

N. T. Wright offers helpful instruction for our missional conversation as he focuses on the source of this hope in his book, *Surprised by Hope*,

> It is the story of God's kingdom being launched on earth as it is in heaven, generating a new state of affairs in which the power of evil has been decisively defeated, the new creation has been decisively launched, and Jesus' followers have been commissioned and equipped to put that victory and that inaugurated new world into practice (Wright, 2008).

Our vision and the vision of our congregations can be found in this commission. Jesus taught us to pray, "Thy kingdom come, Thy will be done on earth, as it is in heaven" (Matt. 6:10 KJV). You and I are being called to be about the business of receiving and entering God's kingdom in this unique time and place. I have come to think of God's kingdom as "shalom space." We are being invited by God's Spirit to enter this space. Here we experience God's peace, justice, and grace.

No one I know lives in this space all the time. Through intentional spiritual formation and discipleship we sometimes realize that it has come near. We can experience the shalom perspective for a time but soon find ourselves back in our more chaotic space. Through these experiences of shalom, we become more prepared to engage in God's mission. The process of intentional spiritual formation is crucial if we are going to respond to the call to missional engagement and spend an increasing amount of our lives in this shalom space.

Incarnational Ministry

"Incarnation is God's ultimate missional participation in human life. The Word was made flesh in Jesus, and the church as the body of Christ must continue to be enfleshed in every human culture and moment in mission. Yet the church's incarnate ministry is not merely an imitation of what Jesus did; it is a participation in a much larger movement in which God is the primary actor" (Van Gelder, 2011).

This missional "enfleshment" provides a different understanding from "doing a mission project" or "going on a mission trip." While the latter may be incarnational, these are more likely to be isolated, stand-alone events focused on a specific task, meeting a particular need, or just a program activity to fill the calendar. Too often such events are undertaken without the theological reflection to challenge participants' views of their being the primary actor in the experience. I am reminded of Jesus' oft-stated phrase, "The kingdom has come near." We can be so close to entering the shalom space of the kingdom but cannot see it because we are focused on the needs that *we* are meeting.

In some congregations we find a convergence of the transitional pressures and the themes of the missional journey. These churches are increasingly finding their identity in God's mission. They are discovering their vision by becoming places where vision can be found.

Perhaps a few stories of what some of these churches are doing will help describe what incarnational ministry looks like. One historic and traditional congregation in Virginia has decided that being the presence of Christ to the refugees in their community requires more than praying for them and hoping for the best. They began to teach English and to provide resources so the refugees could learn whenever they could find time. Previously, the church had offered English classes, but they were scheduled on weekday mornings for the convenience of the volunteer teachers. Refugees working at whatever jobs they could find could not attend. These church folk began to realize that their success was not measured by how many attended their classes but rather by how many learned the English language. Rosetta Stone yellow boxes distributed by the church can be seen in homes across the city as testimony to this missional enterprise.

A congregation in North Carolina had long been a strong supporter of mission offerings. They took pride in setting challenging offering goals and celebrated reaching them. Then another kind of call came. Severe flooding had virtually wiped out a town east of them. Survivors were desperate to get back into their homes. This church responded to the call, and crews of all ages spent weeks and weekends, shoveling mud out of houses. They cleaned and scrubbed. They replaced drywall and became hope for these desperate people. They worked alongside the homeowners and built lasting relationships. When the next disaster struck, they had a ready response. "What can we do to go and be the presence of Christ?"

Four women in one Sunday school class in a church in Atlanta became models of missional living to their entire congregation. They saw a tangible need and determined to do something about it. Women who were completing rehabilitation programs or leaving abusive situations needed a place to begin their way back into society. Often these women have children to care for as they face the task of reentry. The idea of a transition house on the church campus was birthed. These women worked through the administrative process of the church. They shared their vision, got the church's approval, raised money, and enlisted volunteers to remodel the house to make it suitable. Now they are providing emotional and spiritual nurture and care for women and their children who are living in the transitional house.

A congregation in South Carolina has caught the vision of the kingdom of God. They have adopted several mission efforts around the world and are inviting members to invest their money, time, and themselves. One Sunday school group participated in a ministry to a women's prison. During their interactions there they learned that some of the women would intentionally break a rule so their stay in prison would be extended. This seemed to be strange, even counterintuitive behavior. This group learned that many of these women had no place to go when released so they wanted to stay in prison. This group established a nonprofit corporation, raised money, applied for grants, and committed to build a $500,000 halfway house for these women. Perhaps the most symbolic action taken by this church was turning their no-longer-used house for furloughing missionaries into a place for the released prisoners to sleep and have an address.

Another congregation in North Carolina found themselves facing unwanted change. The town in which this church was located had been dominated by the textile industry. The church had enjoyed having several of the executives and managers of these textile mills as members. Almost overnight, it seemed, the mills were closed, and these leaders were gone. The loss of jobs was devastating to the community. Their identity had been so connected to the textile industry that the area struggled even to imagine its future. A group of young parents in this church met each week for fellowship and sharing while their children were in various programs. Their discussion naturally turned to this change and its implications. At first they focused on what this meant for their church, but they soon began to discuss the impact on their church's neighborhood.

For several years the church had provided a summer soccer program for children. The participants had largely been their own children and their friends who played in the church's spring and fall leagues. These parents began to look at the needs in the community and discovered that there were no recreation programs for the children who lived in the area immediately around the church. After some conversations with parents in the neighborhood, this group brought a proposal to the recreation committee that the focus of their soccer program change. And change it did. The church shifted its program to meet this newly identified need in their neighborhood. The program was promoted in the community, and coaches were recruited. That summer more than 100 neighborhood kids joined with the church kids in the church's soccer league. This effort became a symbol for this congregation as they began to live into their role as the people of God in a changing community. For more stories of congregations catching a vision for the kingdom of God, see *Glimpses of Missional Faithfulness*.

Every Member a Minister

"The internal life of the missional church focuses on every believer living as a disciple engaging in mission. The understanding makes every member a minister, with the spiritual growth of every disciple becoming the primary focus as the body is built up to participate more fully in God's mission in the world" (Van Gelder and Zscheile, 2011). Responding to a sending God's invitation, accepting and entering the kingdom of God, and embodying God's mission require intentional discipleship and intentional formation. What do we need to be and do to put ourselves in the best position to participate in God's mission?

In an earlier time we in the church gave our energies primarily to studying about and praying for the faceless, nameless, hungry, homeless, and lost. We called this discipleship. Yes, we often went beyond these activities to giving an offering so someone else could offer hope and direction to these folks. But even in this tradition we find an illustration of our problem. Many churches have historically evaluated their effectiveness primarily by how many attended a study or prayer time and by offerings given. A more telling measure would be how many persons actually experienced the love of Christ because of our efforts. The goal of discipleship must be more than participating in church programs. As an intentional community, the people of God in a unique place and time, we must be about missional discipleship. The goal of this kind of discipleship is to invite persons to hear God's invitation to God's mission and to support and encourage their response.

Discipleship is about responding to the Great Commission, but it is more than that. Discipleship is introducing persons to Jesus, but it is also introducing them to the mission for which Jesus was sent. Consider this definition of spiritual formation: Spiritual formation is the process of being conformed to the image of Christ by the gracious working of the Spirit for the transformation of the world. Sadly, most congregational discipleship programs inoculate members from being conformed to the image of Christ or experiencing God's mission. We too often really mean, "Just be a good church member." The goal of missional discipleship is to assist persons to accept God's kingdom that is coming on earth as it is in heaven and to move into, experience, and offer to others the shalom space of peace, justice, and celebration now, even as they anticipate God's future.

A parable that has been around for years still haunts me, the parable of the pipes. As the story goes, many years ago a group of people discovered a sacred spring deep in the forest. They had been on a desperate search for water when this spring of living water miraculously appeared. Every year the people would make the long journey back to the spring to give thanks for this provision. After a few generations passed, some inventive soul decided to run a pipe from the spring to the center of the village so they would not have to trek to the spring deep in the forest. After a while, only the oldest folk continued the annual ritual of going to the spring to give thanks. Others simply gathered around the pipe in the village. As time passed, younger generations decided that it would be convenient to run the water to each person's home, so an elaborate system of pipes was developed. It was a sight to behold. The elders continued to tell stories they remembered hearing of the provision of the living water. Over time the annual ritual took on a new focus. The people would gather and marvel at the elaborate system of pipes that carried the water to each house. These people started out being thankful for the provision of living water but were now worshipping the pipes!

Unfortunately, many congregations have envisioned measuring the effectiveness of our methods rather than the accomplishment of God's mission. We took great pride in how many attended a mission study and how much offering we received. Our programs became our bottom line rather than God's mission. We worship the pipes; we miss the miracle.

You and I, as followers of Jesus Christ, are being called to "missional messiness." You and I are called to invest in the lives of individuals with the certainty of God's unpredictable results. You and I are called to be the presence of Christ in the lives of individuals so filled with noise that it could be years if ever before they hear the good news. This is not a safe place. This is not an easy challenge. In a word it is messy.

This is what Guder means when he says, "Our challenge is to move from church with mission to missional church" (Guder, 1998). Our challenge is to move from being a church with a missions program to being a church that is the presence of Christ in the world. "*The kingdom has come near.*" We are being invited to receive and to enter.

The invitation to missional engagement calls the people of God to roll up their sleeves and do whatever it takes. Alan Roxburgh in recent years has been saying that God's missional call is a call for us to move back into our neighborhoods (Roxburgh and Romanuk, 2006). God's missional call is not limited just to persons in our city or region. God is a God for all people, even those in the most difficult places and circumstances. Some may be tempted to develop a myopic view of God's mission, to limit God's mission to their passion or their area of the country. We cannot limit God's mission to *our* vision. We are called to care as God cares and to care for those for whom God cares.

Caring as God cares requires a variety of methods. Some among us have expressed the concern that inviting people to missional engagement will have a negative impact on cooperative mission efforts around the world. This should not be the case. The result can be just the opposite. When individuals experience the joy of actually being the presence of Christ for others, they want to make sure missionaries in the hard places where they cannot go can have this same opportunity. When we experience being hope for someone who has lost hope, we want more than ever to share in supporting a system designed to offer that hope to those in such difficult places.

This call to missional engagement may force us to examine our operationalized theology, what our actions say about God. Many Christians operate out of a sense of scarcity. We have only so much money, energy, time, or other resources. We have to be judicious in how we allocate them. While these folks say they believe in an omnipotent, grace-offering God, their actions say otherwise. They act as though Jesus said, "The precipice is near" rather than "the kingdom of God is near."

You and I are to respond to God's call to missional engagement out of a sense of abundance. God has all the resources necessary to accomplish God's mission locally and globally. In this God and this mission we find our hope and vision to offer hope to others. What an opportunity!

CHAPTER 3

Leading in Constant Change

We are in the moving stream of history, so it is crucial that we look outside the walls of the church to understand the world around us and our role in it. The church finds its true self as it discovers how it is to carry out God's mission in its particular context. This is its missional mandate.

The world is changing rapidly. Our culture and context are far different from just a few years ago. The bottom line of institutional measures is no longer a sufficient gauge of our effectiveness as the people of God in the world. Focusing our energies and passions on maintaining the church as an institution is not effective. This does not mean we value the local church any less. As a matter of fact, the local church is needed now more than ever. The problem is not with the critical role of congregations but rather with the vision of many with a focus on the wrong priorities, the wrong bottom line.

This reality brings us to the heart of this work. All congregations are facing significant transition. Congregations and individual Christians are facing a significant crisis of identity. Who are we to be as people of faith in this less friendly, less accommodating culture? How can we move from institutionally driven, clearly defined evaluative criteria to seemingly less precise missional measures? A recent conversation with a lay leader illustrates a part of the challenge.

"Well, if we change our bottom line, how will we know if the pastor is doing his job? How will we know if the church is being faithful? It seems to me, if people are coming and giving their money, they are happy for the most part."

This prevailing perspective calls for a new set of leadership skills to guide the church. In addition to these process skills, leaders are needed to help congregations embrace a compelling vision of its future. To what are we transitioning? How are we being formed and reformed? What is God calling us to be and do at this unique place and time? Discovering the answers to these questions frames the leadership challenges facing congregations today.

Pastors, staff ministers, and lay leaders are being called to shepherd their anxious people into and through these transitions. Congregations are facing a number of specific leadership challenges:

- Seeking vision/direction
- Identifying the various transitions
- Inviting the congregation to the risky transitional journey
- Encouraging the congregation to become involved in God's mission
- Inviting persons to receive and enter the kingdom of God

Congregations are facing seismic transitions unlike anything the church has faced in generations. The foundations of our understandings of church are being shaken. The once safe and dependable space is being threatened.

Current congregational leaders have not been trained to lead this kind of systemic transition. They may have the theological foundation. Most have a depth of spiritual maturity and the desire to go deeper. And many have a love for the church and for its people. While today's congregational leaders are God-called women and men, many do not have the tools necessary to guide the congregation through constant change.

Congregations continue to encourage and nurture God's call to ministry. Many of these "called-out ones" pursue theological education in preparation for vocational ministry. Many are called to ministry positions in congregations, and then the almost inevitable crisis begins.

"These folks are more anxious than I anticipated. Even small issues get blown out of proportion," is how one young minister described her congregation. Unfortunately, it is not just young ministers who are poorly equipped to face this leadership challenge. "I have never seen this congregation so anxious, with such a short fuse," is how one veteran pastor described his congregation. "We have never faced this level of uncertainty, and it shows in how we are treating one another," offers another. This is a pervasive challenge facing congregations and their leaders.

A word of warning needs to be offered at this point. As the transitional challenges become more obvious in a congregation, the pressure increases to find a quick fix. Most of the leader generations in congregations today have been shaped by modernity. Their default is still a production model. They see the attendance numbers. They watch the budget reports. They pay attention to the negative comments they hear. As they experience the anxiety growing in the congregation, their predictable reaction is to fix the problem. They are almost compelled to rescue the church from continued decline and eventual ruin. Often these leaders will point to a neighboring congregation whose production numbers are better. "Why can't we be like that church?" can become the rallying cry for this group.

Any veteran of congregational ministry can name these people. As you read, faces come to mind. These persons are acting out of what we have taught them. What is most important is the mission of the church. If the church is to accomplish its mission, it needs to be strong. They know that for the institution to remain strong, peace and harmony are needed in the fellowship. As these leaders experience the heightened anxiety that is inevitable with the transitions churches are facing today, they fear the worst. They fear that the congregation they have invested their lives in has lost its focus on its mission. Their church has lost its vision. They fear that the way they have always experienced church is ending.

This scenario has been played out in congregation after congregation. These churches and these leaders need to come to a new way of understanding their situation. We are proposing a framework to shape this understanding and pointing to some specific resources to assist congregational leaders in this difficult but critical process.

Three guiding missional questions can frame the key leadership challenges facing congregations today:

- Where are we being called to connect with God's *vision* at this unique place and time?
- What do we need to be and do in order to provide experiences for *spiritual formation* as we participate in God's mission?
- How do we as the congregation, as individuals and ourselves as leaders, claim our calling to be the people of God *engaged* in the world?

Congregational leaders are being given a once-in-several-generations opportunity. Following Drucker, Tickle, and others (chapter 1), we have a once-in-every-500 years or so challenge. Lucky us! We have this rare opportunity to lead congregations to make the transition from a traditional/institutional perspective to missional self-understanding. We have the challenge of leading our congregations to transition from a Christendom understanding of church and mission to embracing our role as the people of God, an instrument of a sending God to accomplish God's mission.

Three specific resources can be beneficial in leading this transitional process. These resources represent the broad areas of transition, adaptive leadership, and missional leadership. These resources are each unique and independent. When woven together, they can inform our journey toward answering the three guiding questions.

The work of William Bridges in his book *Transitions: Making Sense of Life's Changes* speaks to the transition process. Bridges provides a big-picture view of change with his three-movement process. He also clarifies the difference between change and transition.

The work of Ronald Heifetz and his associates, *Leadership Without Easy Answers*, focuses on "adaptive leadership." The specific type of leadership skills and perspectives needed to manage the transitions our congregations are facing are outlined.

Finally, in chapter 4, findings from personal research into effective congregational leadership will be presented. We have identified five qualities that prove valuable to those who are called to lead a congregation through transitions.

First we need a brief overview of these three resources. Then, using the guiding missional questions as our frame, we will weave these three resources together to show how they can inform the many leadership challenges congregational leaders are facing.

Transitional Process

One of the most helpful insights for managing transition of any kind comes from William Bridges in his book, *Transitions: Making Sense of Life's Changes*. Bridges differentiates between change and transition:

> *Change* is your move to a new city or your shift to a new job. It is the birth of your new baby or the death of your father. It is the switch from the old health plan to the new one, or the replacement of your manager by a new one or it is the acquisition that your company just made. In other words, change is situational.
>
> *Transition*, on the other hand is psychological. It is not those events, but rather the inner reorientation and self-redefinition that you have to go through in order to incorporate any of those changes into your life (Bridges, 2004).

Bridges describes the entire process of change and transition as consisting of three sequential movements: *endings, neutral zone,* and *new beginnings.*

First, a system has to experience what Bridges calls "endings." "Considering that we have to deal with endings all our lives, most of us handle them poorly" (Bridges, 2004). Bridges warns that our tendency is immediately to focus on the new things. A key element of a transition is that some familiar, comfortable, previously effective things must come to an end. Circumstances have rendered them no longer helpful or even harmful to the new emerging reality. This is the point where many systems get stuck.

Many congregations cannot hear the call of God to God's mission for the noise created by the need for peace and harmony within the fellowship. Congregations are experiencing endings. Some are seeing the ending of their former size and prestige. Others are finding their homogeneous neighborhoods ending. Many are experiencing the ending of denominational identity and relationship.

The question is not whether we will have endings but rather what will we do with them. This is a challenge for leading in constant change. Endings evoke grief. Many church members are coming to church these days in a defensive posture needing someone to help them through the grief and loss they are experiencing. More often than not, these folk find others who are feeling the same way. Together they look for ways to stop and even reverse these endings. The role of leadership is critical here if the transition process is to continue effectively. Leaders need to find ways to be present with persons and their grief. No good will come by ignoring these strong emotions and hoping these folk get over it.

The second phase is an "in between time." The system needs to experience a time of disequilibrium before moving forward. Here is a time and space for persons to work though their grief and loss. In this time discernment of a new vision can take place. Again, leadership is critical here. Offering a discernment process to the largest possible number of participants is key. Without this experience we leave people at best on the sideline and more often in direct opposition to the church's new future. This *is* a process. Our culture and our congregational systems push us to speed through this process and come up with solutions. Congregations need to create space where they can search the Scriptures and pray together to hear the voice of God. At this point we move into the dangerous place of opening ourselves to the leading of the Holy Spirit. This is a risky place. This is a leadership challenge.

Through this risk-taking those in a congregation can begin to embrace the new world in which they find themselves. Here the focus turns to discovering God's mission and our particular role in that mission. Only then is the congregation ready for Bridges' third movement, "new beginnings."

The third movement begins after acknowledging the changes and resultant grief and after a time of intentional discernment and reflection. Expressing a new understanding of what it means for them to be the people of God in the world is risky. Our past is littered with ministers and churches who tried a shorter route. Ministers have been fired while others have burned out or dropped out. Members have chosen sides to defend their points of view while others have left the church looking for a place that is "a better fit" or has less tension. Churches struggle to find traction and identity. The stakes are high.

Bridges' transition model gives us a helpful way to conceptualize the transition process that all congregations are experiencing. This model also helps highlight some key leadership challenges. In this context of transition, we need to focus more specifically on leadership itself. How do we come to these leadership issues? What resources do we bring to address these almost overwhelming challenges?

Adaptive Leadership

Bridges provides a helpful distinction between change and transition. Change is situational and transition is psychological.

The transitional challenge centers on our response to the changes happening around us and to us.

Ronald Heifetz focuses on the leadership skills needed to navigate this challenge toward a missional reality. Heifetz's work speaks directly to the congregational situations we have been examining. Heifetz's book, *Leadership Without Easy Answers*, opens an entirely new way of thinking about the tasks of leadership. Heifetz suggests that there are two basic types of leadership challenges: technical and adaptive. Each requires a different leadership response.

Technical challenges are generally dealing with change while adaptive challenges are focused on transitions. While you might not be jumping up and down with enthusiasm upon discovering a new leadership theory, a real-life illustration might help you understand its relevance. Heifetz begins by offering a wonderfully clear illustration of the difference in technical and adaptive challenges.

An individual goes to his physician with a problem. The doctor examines him, writes a prescription, and sends the patient on his way. This represents a technical challenge that has a clear solution. However, if this same patient returns to his physician and after extensive tests it is determined that he has a serious heart condition, there is no easy solution. The doctor cannot write a prescription to "fix" the patient's problem. The doctor advises the man to change his lifestyle. He will need to change his diet and begin a regular exercise program if he is to correct this problem. The leadership task is to mobilize the patient to make necessary behavioral changes. This is an adaptive challenge. This is a transition. There are no quick fixes, no magic bullets. A solution requires intentional change on the part of the patient if he is to survive and thrive. Welcome to the transitional process and the resultant challenges facing leaders.

Churches today are facing both technical and adaptive challenges. We are practiced and proficient at dealing with technical challenges. We know how to respond to a leaking boiler or a rotting roof. We know how to organize committees and create annual calendars. We know how to develop programs to address a variety of issues. We are so practiced and proficient and so comfortable in our leadership approach that we may have difficulty recognizing an adaptive challenge when it arises. According to Heifetz, the most common failure stems from trying to apply technical solutions to adaptive challenges (Heifetz, 2009).

Adaptive challenges require adaptive work. Heifetz and Laurie suggest that there are three specific times when adaptive work is required: "When our deeply held beliefs are challenged, when the values that made us successful become less relevant, and when legitimate yet competing perspectives emerge" (Heifetz and Laurie, 1997).

If we are honest with ourselves, every congregational leader I know would say that we are facing these three challenges simultaneously. This is what constant change looks like. "Adaptive work consists of the learning required to address conflicts in the values people hold, or to diminish the gap between the values people stand for and the reality they face. Adaptive work requires a change in values, beliefs, or behavior" (Heifetz, 1994).

We are less practiced and proficient at leading individuals to address the gap between their long-held values, beliefs, and behaviors and those that are called for if we are to be the people of God in the world. This kind of intimate leadership requires a depth of relationship and trust that develops over time and a process that requires time to resolve.

Heifetz and Laurie offer six principles for leading adaptive work (Heifetz and Laurie, 1997). These principles are definable actions that can be practical tools for congregational leaders.

1. *Get on the balcony.* Always keep the big picture of what's going on clearly in focus. Often we are in the midst of the fray and fail to appreciate all that is going on. Leaders need this balcony perspective in order to manage the adaptive process.

2. *Identify the adaptive challenge.* One of the benefits of getting on the balcony is being able to get a clearer view of what is going on. The fundamental adaptive challenge may be hidden in the midst of immediate, technical challenges.

   Using the image of a pressure cooker, Heifetz and Laurie say a leader must first contain the challenge. This begins by clearly identifying the adaptive challenge and keeping it in sharp focus. Inevitably pressure will build in the system, and one of the most difficult tasks of an adaptive leader is to keep the focus and direction on meeting the challenge without allowing the level of distress to sabotage the process.
3. *Maintain disciplined attention.* A leader must keep the process moving to conclusion. Some leaders may not be on board with the process. Some might have more at risk in the transition you are moving toward. For a good result, all the key people must be kept in the process.
4. *Give the work back to the people.* The pastor's job is not to fix the problems. All members must invest in identifying the challenge and be fully invested in the process of finding a solution.
5. *Protect voices of leadership from below.* Many times those who have little or no official position or power go unheard. Often their efforts at being heard are unpolished and ill-timed, but their perspectives can make great contributions in a system filled with leaders who are protecting their own turf.

We are skilled at keeping the machine running. We are comfortable managing programs and calendars. We are less sure when we face these adaptive challenges. These issues, if acknowledged, can pose direct threats to our congregation's fellowship, its peace and harmony. Congregational leaders, both lay and clergy, are in a difficult place. If we acknowledge that our deeply held values are being challenged, we risk exposing a lack of skill to manage the problem while at the same time raising anxiety within the system. In congregation after congregation, leaders are responding to this constant change by either acting as if it does not exist or retreating inside the walls and doing what they have always done with more urgency.

In a later work, *The Practice of Adaptive Leadership* (Heifetz, 2009), Heifetz defines adaptive leadership as the practice of mobilizing people to tackle tough challenges and thrive. Rather than following the path of least disruption, congregational leaders are being called to follow the path that gives their congregation the best possible chance to thrive.

Heifetz suggests some key characteristics of adaptive leadership that can help us here:

"Adaptive leadership is specifically about change that enables the capacity to thrive" (Heifetz, 2009). An obvious leadership challenge is assisting congregations in determining what thriving will look like in one's own context. This is a universal trap for leaders. We almost always have competing visions of what thriving looks like within a congregation. For some this vision harkens to a former time when things were good, while for others it is some idealized future. And for others thriving is when everyone is happy.

A key perspective of this work is that we frame our adaptive challenge by asking the three guiding missional questions. What would our congregation look like if it were fully engaged in God's mission in the world? If we did that, then what would thriving look like? However, let us examine an alternative understanding. A congregation is thriving when it is continually seeking to understand and to live out its role in God's mission in the world. A congregation is thriving when it understands that it is *not* the good news but that it is called to be the presence of Christ who *is* the good news.

Heifetz's second characteristic of adaptive leadership is helpful at this point. "Successful adaptive changes build on the past rather than jettison it" (Heifetz, 2009). The task is not to reject the past and start over; that is both too easy and too costly. Adaptive work calls people to distinguish what is essential to preserve from their church's heritage and what is expendable. Our congregations have been about God's mission all along. We must be careful not to reject our heritage because some of the methods are no longer effective. We must also come to some agreement on which elements of our congregational life are expendable or even harmful to our transition process and to our thriving. One simple evaluative question to guide this process might be: Does this encourage us or distract us from accomplishing our role in God's mission?

Finally, *"adaptation takes time"* (Heifetz, 2009). Technical challenges can be addressed often in a single meeting or even with one phone call or e-mail. We like that! This efficiency makes us feel productive and successful. This approach offers instant gratification. The kind of challenges congregations are facing today require attention over the long haul. To use Heifetz's words, "Progress is radical over time yet incremental in time" (Heifetz, 2009). Leading in such a way requires ministers to invest in their congregations for the long haul. This is a highly relational and deeply intimate process.

A primary assumption of this work is that congregations and their leaders are facing an increasing number of complex transitions and adaptive challenges. Left to their own devices, most congregational systems will treat these challenges as technical problems and rely on existing structures to fix them. We know all too well what the result will be. We may delay the problem temporarily, but the underlying issues remain and will reemerge all too soon. Congregational leaders, both clergy and laity, express growing frustration and heightened anxiety. One statement from Heifetz still rings in my ears: "There is no such thing as a dysfunctional organization because every organization is perfectly aligned to achieve the results it currently gets" (Heifetz, 2009).

This leads to two almost counterintuitive responses for leading congregations through such transition. First, the kind of leadership needed desperately by today's congregations is usually not the kind of leadership they are looking for or want. Adaptive leadership will face resistance and create tension within the congregation. This flies in the face of our need to maintain peace and harmony within the fellowship. Practicing adaptive leadership does not call us to the path of least resistance but hopefully to a more effective future.

Second, practicing adaptive leadership requires leaders to invest for the long haul. This leadership approach calls for a level of trust and depth of relationship that must be nurtured over years of walking through life together. Without this depth of trust, all too often congregations and their leaders refuse to recognize the necessary "endings," Both pastor and people employ a technical fix. The pastor decides to find another congregation that is a "better fit." Congregations want to employ a "savior" to fix their problems with little or no discomfort. "The most common cause of failure in leadership is produced by creating adaptive challenges as if they were technical problems" (Heifetz, 2009).

According to both Bridges and Heifetz, congregational leaders need to encourage or at least allow creative tension to develop and to live with that tension and its results for the long term.

This is obviously not the most popular formula for success and happiness, particularly in the short term. Yet many ministers have discovered that it can be the most satisfying and effective. They have discovered a truth that should be obvious, "If you are not engaged with your own heart, you will find it impossible to connect with theirs" (Hefietz, 2009).

Let's now turn to the third major resource for assisting congregations and their leaders in meeting transitional challenges. The five qualities of missional leadership that have emerged from our own research over the years will be presented in chapter 4.

CHAPTER 4

Qualities of Missional Leaders

One of the emerging themes of the missional conversation is *every member a minister*. A missionary God sends all believers to engage the world and be about God's mission of reconciliation. A pastor I served with years ago had a powerful way of symbolizing this calling. Immediately after baptizing new believers, the pastor would face the newly baptized and place his hands on their head and ordain them to ministry. This is a wonderfully missional act and serves as a powerful reminder of our call to be ministers.

Taking seriously the concept of *every member a minister* has several implications. Two are most pertinent to this discussion. First, if all are called to missional engagement, then the congregation must take discipleship seriously. This theme has implicit intentionality. Ministering in and to the world in which we find ourselves requires more than a calling; this task requires preparation and a community of support.

Discipleship has been a historic function of the church. That function has obviously been influenced by how the church understood mission. As we have discussed previously, God's mission was replaced by the church's mission; therefore, the role of the disciple became focused on helping the church succeed. The measure of discipleship became more evident inside the walls of the church. Participating in the programs and activities of the church became a key measure of discipleship. If you participated *and* supported these efforts financially, you surely were a mature disciple. If, however, our understanding of mission changes, then our expectation of a disciple changes as well.

The missional church today must become a faith-forming, disciple-making enterprise. The curriculum must go beyond devotional Bible study and encouragement to be a good church member. A comprehensive curriculum needs to be offered that invites formation and engagement. Spiritual formation is vital if we are to be in a place to discern and respond to God's invitation to God's mission. Missional engagement puts feet to every member's call to minister and to participate in God's mission in the world. Persons on this discipleship journey need to be guided by a missional theology, informed and shaped by Scripture, and expected to engage their community as the presence of Christ.

Second, *every member a minister* has profound implications for the role of the ordained ministers in the congregation. The expectations of ministers have been long established in the minds of the members. Their roles, while nuanced from congregation to congregation, are mostly unwritten but held closely by the members. Often the current minister will be compared to previous ministers and evaluated by how he or she measures up. Yet, as any congregational leader knows, each congregation has many sets of expectations. Practically all ministers today have job descriptions that spell out their duties and the expectations placed upon them. Each of us could recount stories of a minister who met the requirements of his or her job description carefully but failed to meet the expectations of certain segments or individuals within the congregation. A good job description is a technical answer to an adaptive challenge. As long as the minister's role is seen as primarily pastoral, the challenge is to keep everyone happy, to meet everyone's needs, to take on everyone's burdens. Following Heifetz's advice, we need to "get on the balcony" and see the big picture. The adaptive challenge here is not how the pastor can make everyone happy, but rather how the pastor can lead the congregation to embrace God's mission at this unique place and time. "Instead of looking for a savior, we should be calling for leadership that will challenge us to face the problems for which there are no simple, painless solutions—problems that require us to learn new ways" (Heifetz, 1994).

Alan J. Roxburgh and Fred Romanuk offer an insightful resource contrasting pastoral and missional models for leadership in their book, *The Missional Leader: Equipping Your Church to Reach a Changing World* (Roxburgh and Romanuk, 2006). The chart on the following page articulates the differences in these models.

"You may choose your own description and categories, but the principle is the same: in a situation of rapid discontinuous change, leaders must understand and develop skills and competencies to lead congregations and denominational systems in a context that is missional rather than pastoral" (Roxburgh and Romanuk, 2006).

Wow! If you are, or ever have been, a minister in a local congregation, you can probably feel your own anxiety rising a bit. The "pastoral" model has served us well for generations. This is the model we were both trained in and shaped by. This perspective on the pastor has made its way into the DNA of congregations. This is how a minister should act. This is what we expect.

Roxburgh and Romanuk are suggesting that if a congregation is going to make the transition from a church with a mission to a church as an instrument of God's mission, ministers must also transition in how we lead. This requires a renegotiation of how a minister should act. For most current congregational leaders, the "pastoral" model is our norm. This model closely resembles Heifetz's technical leader.

As you take a closer look at the missional model, you can almost hear the echoes of our previous discussion of adaptive leadership. The authors contrasting "pastoral" and "missional" models of leadership have given us, at least in part, a picture of what technical

Pastoral	Missional
Expectation that pastor be present at every meeting and event or else it is not validated or important	Staff ministers operate as coaches and mentors within a system that is not dependent on them to validate the importance and function of every group by being present.
Ordained ministry staff functions to give attention to and take care of people in the church by being present for people as they are needed (if care and attention are given by people other than ordained clergy it may be more appropriate and effective but is deemed "second-class").	Ordained clergy equip and release the multiple ministries of the people of God throughout the church.
Time, energy, and focus shaped by people's "need" and "pain" agendas.	
Pastor provides solutions.	Pastor asks questions that cultivate an environment that engages the imagination, creativity, and gifts of God's people in order to discern solutions.
Preaching and teaching offer answers and tell people what is right and wrong: • Telling • Teaching • Reinforcing assumptions • Offering principles for living	Preaching and teaching invite the people of God to engage Scripture as a living word that confronts them with questions and draws them into a distinctive world: • Using metaphor and stories • Asking new questions
Professional Christians	"Pastoring" must be part of the mix but not the sum total.
Celebrity (must be a home-run hitter)	
Peacemaker	Makes tension OK
Conflict suppressor or "fixer"	Conflict facilitator
Recovery expert ("make it like it used to be")	Cultivator of imagination and creativity
Functions as a manager, maintainer, or resource agent of a series of centralized ministries focused in and around the building that everyone must support; always seen as the champion and primary support agent for everyone's specific ministry	Creates an environment that releases and nourishes the missional imagination of all people through diverse ministries and missional teams that affect their various communities, the city, nation, and world with the gospel of Jesus Christ

and adaptive leadership looks like in a congregation. This work helps us place adaptive leadership theory into real and practical applications.

Congregational leaders in the twenty-first century are being called on to lead a significant transition on two fronts. First, they are being called to lead the members of the congregation from being good church members to participating in God's kingdom. At the same time, these leaders are having to reimagine their role moving from caring for church members to equipping the people of God for the mission of God.

So a fair question at this point is: Why would anyone choose to go into ministry? I understand. In fact, in an alarming trend across the country, fewer individuals are enrolling in seminaries, and fewer still have interest in congregational ministry. Recently, after participating in a workshop dealing with these issues, a college student offered his perspective. "Now, let me see if I understand. You are saying that I should consider taking three plus years to earn a master's degree and then take a job in a small church that cannot pay very much and then try to lead them to a place where they do not want to go? What a deal!" What a deal indeed! God continues to invite us to accept the gift of the kingdom and to enter in. Some among us are being called to lead the church to accept this gift from a sending God, to experience the "shalom space" of this kingdom and to be sent to proclaim to the world the good news, "The kingdom of heaven is near."

Previously we discussed how the church has been influenced by the production model that determined the church's bottom line. Generations of young adults have also bought into this perspective. Congregations can no longer remain passive in nurturing and developing future leaders. Yes, this is a task to which one must be called. Yet congregations, now more than ever, must be intentional about creating environments where their members can hear and respond to God's call in their lives.

One significant influence for such a nurturing environment of call seems obvious—healthy ministers. Future ministers need to have healthy role models of ministers who are experiencing fulfillment in their calling. They need to see that ministering in a congregation can be a place of deep gladness and not just a place of difficult challenges. These individuals need to be given opportunities both to minister and to receive ministry. Ministers and lay leaders need to affirm this exploration of vocation and provide ongoing encouragement through this journey. Congregations need to be intentional about developing such an environment.

However, the "calling" by itself is not enough. Individuals need support as they prepare to live out their calling. Here is another place for congregations to be intentional. Those who are pursuing God's call need encouragement. They need the prayers of the people. They need to know that their church family believes in them and cares about them. They need encouragement to pursue a theological education.

The delivery of theological education is also changing rapidly. Many new delivery systems are emerging to provide theological education experiences. The traditional, residential institution is still the preferred option of many. Many wonderful schools can provide an excellent theological education. Regardless of the platform, a major and practical issue facing theological students is debt. As a congregation takes seriously its role of nurturing God's call, they can affirm, encourage, and support those whom God calls in a tangible way by assisting with the cost of their theological education through scholarships, grants, loans, or gifts.

Most theological schools require a recommendation from a prospective student's church as a part of the application process. Congregations need to take what has become perfunctory as an opportunity to express tangible support and affirmation. One of the ways congregations can connect with God's mission is by supporting those whom God has called, especially one of their own. As part of this affirmation/recommendation process, the congregation should commit to support this called-out one financially as he or she pursues theological education.

Investing in future leaders is vital, but so is investing in our present leaders. As we have already stated, leading in a time of transition is difficult at best and often discouraging, lonely, and overwhelming. Congregations need to recognize this reality and nurture and care for their ministers with a similar level of intentionality. Friend and colleague, Dave Odom, states the challenge succinctly: "We need to treat our ministers as renewable resources rather than expendable commodities." Many efforts are being made to encourage and support congregational leaders. Congregations play a vital role in this nurturing process.

One of the leaders in this effort to invest in present leaders is the Lilly Endowment. Two of their initiatives in which my work has been directly involved are Transition into Ministry (TIM) and Sustaining Pastoral Excellence (SPE). The TIM initiative focuses on the critical first years of congregational ministry. This is obviously a significant transition time. The Endowment has encouraged and made possible creative efforts at assisting women and men as they discover what ministers need to lead a congregation facing a constant change. Not only are these ministers learning what leadership requires; they are also receiving support and encouragement to help them as they often find themselves in the circumstance described by the college student quoted earlier.

The SPE initiative has given primary focus to encouraging ministers currently serving in congregations to raise their sights from survival and maintenance to a more excellent way. Our efforts in this initiative have tried to create a space where ministers could come together for support and encouragement. Additionally, they are invited to discover and exercise the pastoral imagination necessary for leading the transitions that both the congregations and their leaders are facing. The primary thrust of this effort has been to encourage ministers to gather in peer learning groups to aid in this process.

Congregations should also encourage ministers in living out their calling. They can recognize that the call to God's mission is not just a call to the minister but a call to all the people of God gathered in a particular community. Perhaps we need a third initiative, Every Member a Minister.

Here is the good news. It can be done! It is being done! Ministers and congregations across the country are doing the hard work of understanding their context, managing the transition, and embracing God's mission. Some leaders have been able to navigate these rough waters while others have struggled and failed. Obvious skills, attitudes, and perspectives are crucial in an effective ministry in such a time as this.

A number of questions have shaped my research in this area. Why are some ministers and congregations making the transition to embracing God's mission for a twenty-first-century context? Are some obvious factors present in some pastors that contribute to their ability to lead a congregation to respond to adaptive challenges?

To find answers to these questions, we have conducted personal interviews with 30 pastors. These pastors were chosen because their congregations showed evidence of making progress toward the goal of embracing God's call in their new cultural context. Their churches were well on their way to understanding and becoming missional. These congregations gave evidence of a renewed understanding of their calling to be the people of God in the world.

To be sure, these congregations are "both/and" congregations. That is to say, they are both missional and traditional. These pastors are all serving in long-established congregations. Obviously, these congregational journeys are influenced by many factors beyond the scope of this work. My focus is on the specific role of pastoral leadership in the missional journey of these congregations.

Through observation, reading, research, multiple conversations, and a lifetime of personal experience in congregations, a set of leadership qualities emerged that seemed helpful or even necessary for leaders to express in leading congregations on this journey. With the help of friend and pastor Paul Baxley, five qualities of missional leaders were suggested. Those qualities are:

- Resurrection confidence
- Robust spirituality
- Global perspective
- Heightened curiosity
- Deep love for the church

These leadership qualities exhibited by the pastor contribute positively to a congregation's ability to respond to constant change. These qualities, when expressed by the pastor, contribute to the church's ability and willingness to embrace a new bottom line.

Our questions then became: Are these qualities present in this group of effective pastors? Can they identify these qualities in their lives and ministries? Can they point to some things that encouraged or sponsored the development of these qualities in themselves? Can we learn principles from this cohort that are transferable to others? Let us begin by taking a look at these qualities in some detail. Then we will share some of our findings.

Leadership Qualities Defined

Resurrection confidence—Living out one's vocational life with a vibrant sense that the Christ, who was sent by a missionary God, is alive, present, and working in the congregation and the world. The resurrection is understood in the larger story of God's mission. The resurrection reminds us that God's mission will be realized. When the minister's preaching, teaching, worship leadership, and care for the congregation are informed primarily by the reality of the resurrection, real joy is present. When the empty tomb dictates our vision, captures our imagination, focuses our discernment, and empowers our relationships in the congregation and the community, the ministry is marked by a sure, certain, and well-placed hope.

Robust spirituality—An obvious and growing personal faith, marked by prayer, study, and commitment to spiritual disciplines. Congregants recognize that their minister's life is marked by a vibrant faith, a deeply committed relationship to the risen Christ and are then drawn into the same kind of relationship. At the same time, we suspect that this robust spirituality is the foundation for a sustained and growing pastoral imagination that nourishes a more excellent kind of preaching, teaching, and vision casting for the life of the congregation. Another aspect of this robust spirituality is the minister's awareness of her or his own call journey and willingness to tell the story of that call to the congregation as an illustration of the Spirit's work.

Strong sense of curiosity—Interest in the world and the church and God's work with both. Ministers who bring such curiosity to their teaching and preaching exhibit a deep capacity for wonder and awe and a willingness to embrace mystery and uncertainty. This heightened sense of pastoral imagination compels a deeper commitment to a kind of creativity and study that searches for truth and meaning with a compelling persistence.

Global perspective—A worldview that informs their vision, nourishes their imagination, and pushes them into an ever-widening network of relationships. Increasingly, Christianity is a worldwide movement, and baptism into Christ joins us to a global community. This recognition causes excellent ministers to reject attempts by any nation to make exclusive claims on the love of Christ, while at the same time making such ministers eager to enter into relationships with Christians around the world and to learn from sisters and brothers in faith as much as to teach them. The global perspective that marks excellent ministry also contributes to a missional vision for the minister's work in her or his own congregation.

Deep love for the church—A desire for the church to follow God's mission and a desire to serve God's people. Missional ministers understand the central role of the church in the mission of

God. This is not a love that denies the struggles present in human life but a love rooted both in the love of Christ and in an ongoing awareness of the presence of the risen Christ in the church. It is such a love that allows the minister to work in an ambiguous "both/and" world of missional and traditional perspectives.

Research Methodology

Each pastor interviewed received these definitions prior to the face-to-face interview. They were invited to reflect on these qualities and determine which, if any, they could identify as being evident in their ministries. Every pastor in this study identified at least two of these qualities as present in his or her ministry. Most of the pastors identified three or more qualities.

Participants were also asked to rank the qualities with which they most identified. After they had identified specific qualities, they were asked to rank them according to how strongly they felt these qualities were being expressed in their present congregation. A number value of five was given to the quality with which they most identified to one for the quality with which they least identified. Those findings are as follows:

Deep Love for the Church	102
Global Perspective	82
Curiosity	78
Resurrection Confidence	70
Robust Spirituality	38

Twenty of the 30 participants ranked the quality of a deep love for the church first or second.

A key finding is that our hypothesis was supported. These qualities were present in these ministers whose congregations show tangible evidence of becoming missional. Additionally, these ministers agreed that these qualities made significant contributions to their leading in this transition process.

Missional Leadership Qualities Expressed

Each minister identified leadership qualities evident in their ministry and illustrated their expression. Some of their responses are shared below.

Resurrection Confidence

The initial reaction to this quality was: Hmm, I've not thought of it that way, but I like the way you have said it. The pastors interviewed were quick to agree that just such a confidence, rooted in the gospel, was vital to facing the challenges before them. Over and over these pastors shared that this confidence was most evident in their preaching and their pastoral care. When their preaching was clearly grounded in the life, death, and resurrection of Jesus as the ultimate source of hope, they felt a deeper connection with God, God's mission, and the congregation. In a time of difficulty or heightened anxiety, these pastors discovered that finding hope in something more certain than the traditions they have inherited or the management skills they have learned was essential.

One pastor shared this experience. "A young woman spoke to me on her way out of the worship service. She asked me directly, 'Do you really believe that Jesus died for me?' I replied, 'Of course I do.' The woman then embraced me and began to weep. Through her tears she finally was able to ask, 'You are not telling me this just to make me feel good are you? Do you really mean what you said in the pulpit?' I assured her that I meant it." He went on to share how this woman had experienced a number of difficulties and had lost all hope. His resurrection confidence offered a connection she desperately needed.

A word that kept coming up in my interviews around this quality was authenticity. This resurrection confidence must be born out of deep conviction and held equally by head and heart. "You can't preach what you don't believe," is how one pastor expressed it. Such authenticity allows for consistency of word and deed. Another pastor put it this way, "If you do not believe it, you cannot live it. And if you do not live it, you cannot expect people to follow."

Robust Spirituality
While the fewest number of participants identified this quality as one of their strongest, every participant said that this quality should be more evident in his or her life. These ministers mirror the larger community where the awareness of spiritual need is not matched with the necessity of discipline. Here again we see a result of our bottom-line production thinking. Developing a robust spirituality takes time and space, which are at a premium.

Some pastors spoke of a sense of emptiness or a feeling of the well running dry. For some, however, this was a leading quality. They spoke of discovering the need to discipline their weekly schedules. If something had to be postponed or eliminated from their schedules, these pastors made sure their prayer and reflection time was not sacrificed. One pastor said that the effectiveness of her preaching was directly tied to her practice of the spiritual disciplines.

Beyond the weekly routine, several pastors had found spiritual retreats to be of great benefit. Setting aside several days to be still, quiet, and vulnerable to God's Spirit had been significant in the lives of most of these pastors. One pastor confessed that he had discovered a disturbing pattern as he thought about this leadership quality. He realized his focus on his spirituality seemed to surface when he was facing a major challenge. He said he felt like the kid who prayed only when the test was really difficult. Several of these pastors indicated they had members of their congregations who modeled robust spirituality and served as encouragers for their own journeys.

Strong Sense of Curiosity

This quality produced the most hesitation and discomfort as the conversations began. Yet it ranked third out of the five qualities in the final tally. Some did not see how curiosity connected with leadership, while others thought of it as somewhat fanciful. Upon further conversation the value of this quality began to emerge. When asked what they were curious about, their perspective began to change.

As a group, these pastors were energized by their curiosity about the world, the church, and how God's mission impacts both. They exhibited a great thirst for learning. Practically all were avid readers, and most were equally avid movie and Internet fans. While they represented a wide range of tastes in literature, movies, and websites, they focused much of their learning and experiencing to the same end: How does this help me and my congregation understand more clearly our role in God's mission in the world?"

Global Perspective

We understand when someone says that our world is shrinking. The phrase "global village" is becoming less a poetic phrase and more a daily reality. As indicated earlier, one of the great transitions churches are experiencing is the changing ethnic makeup of their communities. Combine that with the constant barrage of worldwide news and access to websites from every corner of the earth, and we are faced with the fact that we are living in a different world.

This group of missional pastors is embracing this new reality. They seem to find energy and excitement that different language groups are showing up in their neighborhoods. Several have led groups from their congregations to experience firsthand being the presence of Christ in a different culture. Through mission trips, getting to know a specific people group, or joining a community of missional practice, these pastors are making sure their congregations strive for a balance between caring for one another and caring for the world.

Deep Love for the Church
Every pastor interviewed identified this quality as one they exhibited. One obvious response to this quality was that if ministers did not love the church, they could not stay in ministry. Some told stories of fellow seminarians who burned out during their first or second pastorate. One pastor said, "They did not love the church enough to overlook some of its faults." Another pastor offered this qualification: "I have a deep love for the church, but some congregations I'm not so sure about!" This illustrates a key truth from the discussion of this quality. These pastors have such a strong love for and belief in the church that they are able to deal with the specific weaknesses in their particular congregations. Another put it this way, "Church is similar to family; we start out loving one another and work hard at learning how to like one another."

Sponsoring Agents of Missional Leadership Qualities

In addition to verifying the value of these qualities of missional leadership, we wanted to discover helpful patterns that had encouraged the development of these qualities in the lives of each minister. After these ministers had identified specific qualities as being present in their ministries, we asked them to consider what or who had encouraged the development of that quality.

Resurrection Confidence
Two themes were clearly formative for this quality among the sample. First was their formal theological education. All of these pastors pointed to their seminary experience in helping develop a perspective that could form and hold their faith. Many additionally included their continuing study as important.

The second sponsoring theme for this confidence was the testimony of individuals. These testimonies took the form of congruent lives. Story after story was shared of persons whose life and faith matched. These persons had such a faith confidence that they ordered their lives accordingly. These living testimonies were great encouragement and examples of authenticity for these pastors.

Robust Spirituality

Several pastors talked about the difficulty of making time to address their spiritual lives. With demands on their time and energy, some indicated their spiritual lives could be charted from crisis to crisis. Only when confronted with a major challenge did they turn to find spiritual strength. The word *balance* was used over and over to describe the challenge of maintaining a robust spirituality. Some longed for a more disciplined approach to their spirituality. The pastors interviewed longed for a rhythm in their ministries that fed their professional, spiritual, and personal lives.

Several experiences were suggested that had enriched this quality in their lives. Three pastors said they had been granted a sabbatical, and they dedicated a portion of that experience to their spiritual lives. They included such things as time in a monastery, a private retreat with prescribed reading and reflection, and participation in a spiritual academy as helpful tools.

Strong Sense of Curiosity

The primary sponsoring agent for this quality was missiological. These pastors were all committed to leading their congregations to connect with God's mission in the world. Therefore, they were constantly curious about what that mission looks like and where the connecting points are in their neighborhoods and beyond. That curiosity often took them to places well outside the comfort zones of their congregations.

Global Perspective

Several factors seemed to contribute to the development of this quality. Many shared stories of first learning about far-away places as children in missions programs. They heard stories of missionaries and different countries at an early age. Every one of these pastors had traveled internationally. Their perspective had been broadened beyond their particular communities.

An observation about cultural context is helpful at this point. It would have been most unusual in earlier generations to find a cohort of pastors who had traveled so widely. Additionally, this group was all reared with television. The oldest of this cohort had a TV in his home as a child. This generation has had the opportunity to be globally influenced more than any other.

Deep Love for the Church

Most of these pastors identified a positive church experience as children and youth. They were nurtured, loved, and called into ministry by their congregations. Many referenced a key adult during their formative years. More often this was a layperson serving as a teacher or a youth worker. Three pastors mentioned a youth minister who was significant in their lives.

Family also played a big role. Practically all of these pastors were a part of a family that was active in and committed to a local congregation. A constant theme in their stories was relationships. This group had meaningful relationships in the church. These relationships ranged from peers to pastors. Many told stories of falling in love with the church as they observed the way their pastor loved them and their congregation.

• • •

Leading the people of God in the twenty-first century is a daunting task. Leading the church to make the transition from the comfort of Christendom to the discomfort of not-yetness may be the minister's most formidable challenge. Understanding the process of transition is a good beginning step. The tools of adaptive leadership and the missional model of leading offer some practical handles. Finally, the qualities of missional leadership provide something of a mirror for all of us to use to evaluate what we each personally bring to the leadership task before us.

Over the next three chapters we will examine First Church and some of the transitions they face. Hopefully you will be able to identify some specific challenges your congregation is facing and find encouragement and resources that will assist you and the leaders in your congregation.

PART 2

Applications and Resources for a Missional Reality

CHAPTER 5

Changing Role in the Community

To provide a structure for thinking about this transition, three guiding missional questions frame our leadership challenges. These questions represent the three key components of a comprehensive congregational curriculum:

VISION • FORMATION • ENGAGEMENT

VISION—Where are we being called to connect with God's mission at this unique place and time?
FORMATION—What do we need to be and do to put ourselves in the best position to participate in God's mission?
ENGAGEMENT—How do we offer the invitation to the congregation, to individuals, and to ourselves as leaders to claim our calling to be the people of God in the world?

These guiding questions provide a missional framework for leading the transition process. These questions will force us to deal with difficult issues. They can keep us honest as pastor and people as we do the difficult work of leaning into God's future together. These are our "balcony questions." These questions call us to a missional perspective and can serve as a guiding star when we find ourselves lost in the angst of agendas and the morass of the mundane.

Now we are in the "so what" time. We have described the situation. We have offered resources to assist us as congregational leaders. What difference this makes depends on you and your congregation. So let us return to First Church for a moment. First Church is a fictional congregation that is a composite of many. The following narrative will focus on specific issues this congregation is facing in the three areas of church and culture, the mission of God, and leadership.

What follows is not intended to be a process model to be followed. The intent here is to illustrate how the ideas, concepts, and perspectives we have discussed can intersect with the real issues that face your congregation.

Welcome Back to First Church

First Church was established in 1868 in the midst of a devastated postwar South. Most of the church's history has mirrored that of its environment. First Church struggled and survived primarily due to the real sacrifice of a few committed folk. Throughout its history the congregation has occupied numerous buildings at two different locations. In 1953 the church moved from a land-locked space in the center of town to a large tract just north of downtown.

A key part of this congregation's story is that it continues to mirror its surrounding community. The church's position in the community has changed, however. This did not happen overnight but slowly and almost imperceptibly. Fifty years ago First Church experienced a most traumatic and formative time when members reflected the full range of perspectives evident during the civil rights movement and the struggle for integration and equal rights for all persons. The leaders had genuinely mixed feelings. Some were ready to march while others wondered why things couldn't stay as they were. Sadly, First Church, like so many other congregations at this time, focused primarily on the institution. The question was not, What would God have us do? but rather, What do we do if a black person tries to attend our church?

As the civil rights struggle gained momentum, changes began to happen in First Church. A key layperson began to challenge the church's position and perspective. One by one a growing number of folk became involved in discussing what the church should do. This was an informal process buoyed more by events happening in the community and nation than by the congregation's leaders. First Church was caught between its past and an emerging reality. Finally in 1972 the church revised its bylaws allowing church membership for all persons.

This issue is a good example of the church facing a transition and acting as if it were a simple change. The technical fix was to station ushers at the doors to keep black persons from entering worship. The adaptive response that resulted in a change in attitude of the members took over a decade to be brought to fruition and unfortunately is still not realized in some members.

A more recent crisis came in 1991 when Jane Williams, who had grown up in the church, requested ordination. The church had celebrated her earlier announcement that she was responding to God's call and wanted their endorsement to attend seminary. Jane had completed her studies and had been called to a church in another city. First Church had never ordained a woman. As far as they knew, no church in the city had done so. Fortunately the leadership took a more active role in this situation.

The technical solution to this problem was simple: make sure you have the votes you need at the congregational business meeting. The pastor and key lay leaders were willing to move forward on this issue as the right thing to do even though there was some vocal opposition. The church voted to ordain Jane by a 70 to 30 percent vote. Some voted yes because they affirmed Jane and her call; some voted yes because they believed God can call male and female. Others voted yes hoping the arguing and tension would go away. Jane was ordained, and four families left the church due to their opposition to this action.

First Church again finds itself facing a crisis. Unlike the two previously discussed, this one is less defined. No single issue seems to be commanding the church's focus to fix things. Yet the congregation and ministers feel a palpable sense that something is wrong. Things are not as they used to be. First Church is a midsize congregation that has seen its weekly worship attendance drop from 540 to 389 over the last 10 years. The church has seen a corresponding drop in participation in all program areas. The community population has been stable with a slight increase over this same period. While the population number has remained stable, the ethnic makeup is different. The local school system reports a 30 percent increase in minority enrollment over the last 10 years.

This increased diversity in student population is one reason the local high school no longer uses First Church's sanctuary for their graduations. In the past First Church hosted a variety of community events. Members of the larger community and city leaders were in and out of First Church's facilities on a regular basis. Most of these activities have found newer, more suitable spaces and have moved on.

Budget receipts also reflect the decrease in participation. The church has a ministerial staff composed of a pastor, minister of music and worship, minister of formation and administration, minister of youth, and a music associate/organist. Along with personnel costs, physical plant costs continue to increase and now these two expenses account for 81 percent of the annual ministry budget.

First Church has a facility that can accommodate a weekly attendance of 800. Most of the buildings were built when the church relocated in 1953. These buildings have provided well for the congregation, but now their systems are breaking down. Roofs seem to need repair annually. The exterior needs painting. The maintenance staff has to nurse some air handlers to function on a weekly basis. The light fixtures in the hallways provide an inadequate welcome, especially for visitors.

For several years the finance committee has struggled with reducing program budgets, delaying building maintenance, reducing missions giving, and even reducing the size of the ministerial staff. Several attempts have been made to increase the offerings for the church budget. All of these efforts involved some promotional campaigns to convince members to give more than they gave the previous year. These efforts have not succeeded.

Four years ago a new church was established four miles north of First Church. No one gave it much thought in the beginning. *Who would want to go to church in a warehouse?* seemed to be the general attitude. Then, however, two faithful families with teenagers started attending this new church. Soon several other families followed from First Church as well as from neighboring congregations. This four-year-old "warehouse church" now has four times the attendance of First Church.

A second group applied for a zoning permit to build a place of worship just south of town. The group wanted to build a mosque to serve the growing Islamic community. Some First Church members could not believe this was happening in their community. They joined the petition drive to deny the zoning request. Finally, after much public debate, the request was granted, and the mosque was built. The ground was shifting. The world was changing and could no longer be ignored. The members of First Church were growing increasingly anxious and concerned. They still want to be *First* Church, but what does that mean today?

Pastor Bill Smith was feeling both the increasing anxiety and the pressure to fix the problems at First Church. He participated in all the finance committee meetings. He preached to an ever-growing number of empty pews on Sunday morning. He listened as the remaining youth parents wanted programs and events to keep their kids interested. Comments from longtime members about how things used to be always seemed to be playing in the background. The pastor led weekly staff meetings where the staff expressed their growing frustration with trying to maintain all their programs with less budget support and fewer attending. In each case, many technical fixes were suggested: Cut all budget line items by 20 percent. Establish a visitation program like we used to have. Include music in worship the youth would enjoy.

Pastor Smith has seen this before. Similar factors began to surface in his last pastorate. He had faced no major controversies in his four-year tenure there, but he saw storm clouds gathering. It was certainly a time of mixed emotions for him. Pastor Smith had learned to love his parishioners, but they were becoming increasingly needy, and he did not know what to do. The church members were looking to him for answers he did not have. Then, due to the recommendation of a friend, he received a call from the pastor search committee at First Church. First Church seemed to be in a better place. They were meeting their budget, and everyone seemed excited about the future. Moving to this larger and more promising place was not a difficult decision for Pastor Smith.

This pastor's relocation is a good example of the multilayered transition process. During the last century a pastor could make such a move, and it could be viewed as merely a change. The pastor changed location, and the church changed pastors. In a time of great transition, however, simply making a change is not enough. Pastor Smith thought that by changing locations he could avoid the church's transitional traumas. First Church thought that bringing in a new pastor would ensure their successful future. What often develops is something of a codependent relationship between pastor and people. Both parties want to maintain the familiar, the comfortable. One obvious downside of such a relationship is that when the familiar and comfortable are threatened, the pastor-people relationship can be threatened at a fundamental level. The most obvious and often chosen solution is for the pastor to move on to a new relationship with a different congregation. The congregation, then, looks for "just the right person" to lead them (this being interpreted as maintaining the status quo if not reclaiming our former glory). This is a clear illustration of applying a technical solution to an adaptive challenge.

The good news is that many have lived in this era of transition long enough to recognize the pattern we have just described and realize that it is not a viable answer. Pastor Smith is in that place. While he is unsure of the future and of a process to get there, he is clear that just moving on to another church is not the answer. He is equally convinced that just doing all the things the church is currently doing with more enthusiasm and creativity is not the answer. Driving home late one evening after a particularly difficult church council meeting, Pastor Smith began asking those inevitable and dangerous questions: "Is this what God called me to do? How do I find that passion I had when I responded to God's call on my life? How do you pastor such an anxious people? Can I still be their pastor? *Should* I be their pastor?"

Pastor Smith and First Church are at a pivotal point. Pastor and people need to realize that what they are facing is more than an ordinary cycle of change. Both pastor and people need to be clear that this is much more than change; this is a challenge of transition. William Bridges helps us here: "One of the most important differences between change and transition is that changes are driven to reach a goal, but transitions start with letting go of what no longer fits or is adequate for the life stage you are in" (Bridges, 2004).

Often an anxiety-producing task for a congregation is to identify endings to determine what is no longer adequate for where the congregation finds itself. An even more difficult task is publicly acknowledging these endings and the fears they evoke. A resulting task of the acknowledgment of these endings is to avoid the pressure to offer quick solutions. Remember, we want persons to transition. They must experience and live with the dissonance for a while before they can move psychologically and emotionally to explore new beginnings.

As you read the story of First Church and see how they respond to transition in the areas of mission and leadership, I encourage

you to make a list of the possible endings your congregation might be facing. Some of the more obvious endings First Church is facing regarding its relationship with culture are:
- Place of respect and deference in the community
- Homogeneous neighborhood
- Social and gender roles
- Traditional family systems
- Loyalty to church expressed in time and money
- Singular view of worship
- Purpose and value of long-established programs
- Role of the pastor
- What it means to be a member of First Church

As a congregation enters this transition from institutional to missional, the case has been made that the five qualities of missional leadership will be helpful for all their leaders. If these leadership qualities are limited to the clergy, however, they are reinforcing the institutional model from which they are trying to transition.

REFLECTING ON YOUR CONTEXT

Identity Needs

List endings your congregation is facing.

How will the anxiety produced from these endings likely be expressed?

What are the likely responses when these anxieties are expressed?

What are the technical and adaptive leadership challenges at play in First Church?

What are the technical and adaptive leadership challenges at play in your congregation?

Five Qualities of Missional Leadership

- Resurrection confidence
- Robust spirituality
- Heightened curiosity
- Global perspective
- Deep love for the church

How could these leadership qualities be helpful to First Church?

How do you see these qualities expressed in your congregation?

CHAPTER 6

From Missions Toward Missional

Life and ministry were beginning to change for Pastor Smith. He had participated in a peer group since he came to First Church. This group had been a great source of support and encouragement. For the past year the group has been exploring the wide range of missional literature. For several weeks Pastor Smith's peer group had been discussing *The Missional Leader: Equipping Your Church to Reach a Changing World* by Roxburgh and Romanuk. They had explored what this kind of leadership might look like and what possible reactions one could expect from the congregation. It had become clear to him that he wanted to become more of a *missional* leader than a *pastoral* leader. He was also sure that this was what First Church needed him to become. Bill Smith began by focusing on one question: "How can I shift from providing answers to asking questions that invite the people to come up with solutions?" He wrote that question on an index card and placed it on his desk by his phone where he would be challenged by it daily.

Great relief comes with taking off the role of total responsibility for the congregation. Pastor Smith began to see how this new way of understanding his role as leader began to change him in surprising ways. He had let the congregation assign this responsibility to him, and he had accepted it as part of the job of pastor. From this new place of self-understanding, Pastor Smith began to see individual church members differently. When Wilma Adams, director of the women's mission organization approached him, he was not as anxious as usual. Previously, it seemed that whenever they met, she needed him to fix some problem. "How was he going to promote the mission offering? Why did the staff not seem to be more supportive of this program? Can't you do something to get the younger women to participate?" While Wilma still sees the pastor as "Mister Fix-It," Pastor Smith is beginning to see Wilma differently. He can see more of her passion and commitment rather than focus on her neediness.

He almost surprised himself when he encountered Wilma. She came in with the determined look of a woman who had the total responsibility of saving the entire world. She began with her usual concern about getting more young women to participate in the mission program. After listening to her concern, Pastor Smith said, "Wilma, you are right. More people of all ages should be more involved in missions. Why don't we put this on the agenda for the church council meeting next week? Perhaps we can start a discussion with some of these young women and see what they think about this." Wilma was pleased. The pastor acknowledged her and her concern. He did not give her the answer but offered to give it to the right folk to pursue.

Pastor Smith felt good that he had not assumed responsibility for fixing the problem Wilma had brought. A growing awareness of his own calling and its connection to God's mission was inviting him to ask new questions. If we are being called to join in God's mission, we need to ask some different questions. The question had been: "How do we get more people to participate in our mission programs, and why won't the young women participate in our mission organizations?" During his daily reflection Pastor Smith found a different question emerging: "Where are we being called to connect with God's mission at this unique place and time?" It seemed to him that they were focusing on the wrong bottom line. They were measuring attendance at meetings and amount of money given. They could do all this and still not respond to God's call to participate in God's mission in the world. This was a watershed insight for Pastor Smith, and he realized again that this transition was going to take time for him and the congregation.

As Pastor Smith went about his many responsibilities, the question, "Where are we being called?" was never far from his mind. This new awareness showed up during that week's staff meeting. For some time the staff had been discussing the growing refugee population in their town. They had designated a portion of their missions offering to an ecumenical ministry with the refugees, but that was the extent of the church's involvement. The conversation generally ended with the realization that the church did not have the money to provide any additional assistance. At this point, almost in frustration, Pastor Smith asked, "Do we know what the specific needs of these people are?" No one knew for sure. The minister of formation and administration volunteered to do some research on the specific needs of these new members of the community. She contacted the agency that was most directly involved with these persons. She learned that they had a wide range of needs. One immediate need was for furniture and clothing. Beyond the basic physical needs, these new community members needed language skills in order to find employment. They needed people to walk alongside them and help them with the many unfamiliar things that came their way.

Focusing on the question, "Where are we being called?" put a different light on this need. Pastor Smith then began to think of other important questions: "What do we need to be and do in order to put ourselves in the best possible position to participate in God's mission? How do we address the needs we have discovered?" Simply attending a mission program will not meet these needs. The minister of formation and administration e-mailed this newfound information about the refugee population to all Bible study groups and asked them to make these needs a matter of prayer. Pastor Smith invited a representative group from the young adult

Bible study classes to attend the upcoming church council meeting. He wanted them to have an opportunity to respond. Pastor Smith realized that this was not exactly what Wilma Adams had in mind. But he hoped she would be thrilled to see these needs met in the community.

A change in how they think about missions was being introduced. Obviously, that was not verbalized. All were being invited to experience why a new way of thinking was necessary. A transition to an understanding that missions is both supporting others and personal involvement will take time. Wilma was being invited to learn the lesson Pastor Smith was learning. We must encourage our members to do more than be good church members. We have to address the adaptive challenge of inviting church members to claim their calling to be the people of God in the world. This transition process will take years of intentional focus and a wide variety of mission engagement opportunities around the world.

Perhaps another ending has been identified. For generations the women of First Church had functioned primarily out of a strong program model. It looks much the same as it always had. Missions was their focus as they met for a monthly, daytime meeting. This group did much to promote mission offerings and prayer support. In recent years they experienced a steady decline in participation and in mission support.

For the foreseeable future, mission at First Church will be a both-and proposition. The church will continue to offer traditional mission programs for all ages. They will learn about missions and missionaries. People will be encouraged in the discipline of praying for the entire missions enterprise. First Church will build on its strong tradition of mission support as it encourages individuals and groups to respond to the framing missional question: "Where are we being called to connect with God's mission at this unique place and time?"

The previously mentioned church council meeting illustrates some first steps in such a transition. The goal mission organization leaders present at this meeting expressed was getting young women involved in the mission programs. The alternative missional perspective at work here was to present a tangible need in the neighborhood and see if anyone would respond.

The need for English language education among the recently arrived refugee community was presented. The finance chair quickly offered that they had already overspent the mission budget. Wilma Adams had been discussing this need with the women's mission organization leaders. She offered to provide an ESL class as a part of their monthly meeting at the church.

Finally, Gwen Johnson spoke up. Gwen was a member of one of the young adult classes Pastor Smith had invited to join in the conversation. Gwen began: "I've been praying about this need ever since it was brought to our attention and we were invited to this meeting. A group from our class has been praying and talking about what we could and should do. I talked with the folks at Cooperative Ministries to find out more about these people and their needs." Well, this was not a typical church council discussion!

Gwen continued: "Our class has decided that we would like to work to meet some of these needs. A couple of us have visited with some of the refugee families. The children are in school, and the parents are doing whatever they can to provide for their families. Some work long hours; several work a night shift and try to get some sleep during the day. They keep saying to us as clearly as they can: 'We want to learn English.'"

John, Gwen's husband, picked up here. "We started by thinking of offering traditional ESL classes. As we had further conversations, we realized that would not work. There is no convenient time for such a class for this group. They do not have the transportation options to get to a class, and they do not want to leave their children unattended if one of the parents is working at the time a class would be offered."

"Then this idea came to me," Peggy James broke in. "I had needed a crash course in Spanish for a business trip a few years back.

My company provided a software program for me to use. It was great. I could work on my Spanish whenever I had the time. It was available to me 24-7. All you need is the software, a computer, and motivation."

"That's all well and good," Wilma replied, "but these people can't afford the software, and I am sure that they do not have computers."

"That's right, Wilma," came Gwen Johnson's response. "That stumped us for a while too. But during our prayer time last Sunday, I had a thought. We have an old computer in the closet. I didn't want to throw it away so I kept it. I shared this with the class, and three other families also have old computers. We believe we could find computers for these 15 families The software would cost $225 per family. I've done some checking, and I think we can get a volume discount that would bring the cost down to $200 per family."

"Sounds like we need to have a fund-raiser," Wilma offered.

"We thought about that," Gwen replied, "but we would like to propose a different approach. We would like to invite our folks to adopt one of these families. Yes, we would want them to purchase the software for the family. But more than that, we want to encourage our families to get to know these refugee families. Each family has unique circumstances. Some need basic furniture and clothing. Others need networking to find employment. Children may need tutoring with their schoolwork."

Peggy James then added, "We have an opportunity to live our faith, to be the presence of Christ that Pastor Smith has been preaching about. I want to help these people move from being refugee families to being our neighbors."

Pastor Smith was amazed. He was feeling a renewed excitement about discovering what God was doing in the world. At the same time he did not want to discount the church's mission organizations or persons involved in them. He recognized that a singular perspective on missions was ending at First Church. As a matter of fact, it had ended several years ago, and now it was time to acknowledge it.

The longtime members who had faithfully led the mission programs needed to have time to live in the "in between" time. They did not need to feel discounted but to be lovingly and consistently invited to a new perspective and new ways of engaging.

Each transition an organization or an individual faces brings new opportunities as well as new challenges. Classes and individuals began to respond to a new sense of permission to find creative ways to meet the needs around them. One challenge that became evident for Pastor Smith and First Church was in the area of theological understanding. Several conversations with members helped the pastor recognize this problem. In an earlier day practically everyone had attended a church or grew up in a similar church. That was no longer the case. First Church found itself in a different context. Some of the young adults involved with the refugee families had little or no background to connect their actions with God's mission.

Pastor Smith and the staff realized that an effective transition toward missional engagement would be tied to the spiritual maturity of the individual members. While this was another challenge, it was also a wonderful opportunity. Many individuals of a wide variety of ages were energized by participating in hands-on mission efforts. The staff saw this new interest as an excellent entre into more purposeful discipleship opportunities. Missional engagement and intentional formation must go hand in hand, each illuminating and supporting the other.

The leaders realized that the old assumptions about Bible knowledge, theological understanding, and the role of the church were no longer holding, particularly among the newer members. Pastor Smith realized that if they encouraged people to be the presence of Christ, they needed to know how that looked. If the members of First Church were going to discover their role in God's mission, they needed an intimate knowledge of the God who was sending them and the mission to which they were being called. The move toward *missional* meant that it was no longer enough for the pastor alone to have this knowledge. The locus of responsibility needed to shift from *pastor* to *pastor and people*. Spiritual formation for all ages must become the primary focus and be approached with renewed urgency.

Pastor Smith and the staff began conversations about how spiritual formation was supported by the various programs and activities of the church. They interviewed the young adults who were involved in the English language project. Not surprisingly, they discovered a wide range of understandings. Some were well versed in God's mission and the challenge of representing Christ. Others had little or no theological reference; people needed help, and they were helping. The "church talk" was foreign to them. Other groups, who were longtime church members, could give all the correct answers regarding God's mission and what it meant to follow Christ but were not engaged in any hands-on ministry.

First Church found itself dealing with one of the by-products of Christendom—proxy faith. With its focus on building the institution, the Christendom era offered others to serve as faith proxies. The bottom line for many congregations was the strength of the institution. That focus called for certain things from the members. They needed to be faithful in attendance, constant in giving, and prayerful for the clergy and the missionaries. Although it was unintentional, for many, theirs became a proxy faith. The clergy became their proxies when it came to biblical understanding and spiritual insights. Missionaries became their proxies for connecting with God's mission in the world.

First Church was facing an adaptive challenge focused on its discipleship efforts. Whether its members have a proxy faith background or no faith background, the challenge is the same. How can the church create an environment where individuals can hear and respond to God's call and God's mission? How does the congregation transition from being good church members to being the people of God about God's mission in the world?

The initial response of the staff to this emerging realization was to find a strategy to "fix" everyone by offering technical solutions. What Bible study curriculum can we find that everyone can use? What sermon series should Pastor Smith plan? What programs should be offered? Who else was struggling with this issue? What were they doing?

The members of First Church were facing transition at a fundamental level. How do they understand their personal relationship with God, one another, and the world; and what does that understanding call them to be and do?

The traditional, literature-driven Bible study where everyone participates in the program was ending. Groups at First Church were at different points on the transition continuum. For some this approach had been a lifelong experience. They depended on the structure of the literature and their particular Bible study class. This group would be invited to discussions about the different approach but were welcome to continue in their more familiar pattern if that is what they preferred. The adaptive challenge for this group was not changing their approach to Bible study but to make the connection between their Bible study class and God's mission and to bless others as they chose the best path for their own spiritual formation.

For others, the traditional approach had ended some time ago, while still others had never experienced this programmatic approach. Their adaptive challenge was not forcing everyone into a specific approach but to help them make the connection between their spiritual formation and their role in God's mission.

In the past a committee or council would have brought a recommendation for how First Church would structure the spiritual formation program. After several conversations among Pastor Smith, the ministerial staff, and lay leaders, a perspective began to take shape. The adaptive challenge identified was to find ways to put First Church and its members in the best possible place to thrive. Thriving was seen by this group as hearing and responding to God's call and engaging in God's mission in the world. These leaders were well aware that this was not the picture of "thriving" many church members would offer. They were also aware that an intentional spiritual formation process was one of the critical tools in addressing this adaptive challenge.

Another significant insight began to develop from these conversations. This formation process was not something the pastor and staff had to program and provide. This was a journey that both clergy and laity were being invited to join. The responsibility for spiritual formation rested with each person. Just as each person was accountable to respond to God's call, they were equally responsible to put themselves in the best possible position to hear that call.

The role of church leaders was not to offer one-size-fits-all discipleship programs to fix the problem. The leadership task was to foster an environment where individuals were urged to stay focused on their relationship with God and its meaning in their lives.

What does such a process look like, and how do you manage it? wondered Pastor Smith. He thought: *It seems as though we have to provide individual customization.* Everyone is on his or her own path. Rather than meeting around a prescribed Scripture text, the idea of shared conversations on the journey began to take shape among the leadership team. Many of the adults at First Church were more comfortable starting with their experiences and then having some guidance to connect these experiences to Scripture. This was much easier for them than starting with a Scripture passage they sometimes did not fully understand and then trying to make a connection to their life experience.

This obviously required leaders who had a strong grasp of the biblical story and could help others make appropriate connections. While they were not at all sure how they were going to pull this off, they sensed that they were facing the adaptive challenge of moving from efficiency to effectiveness in the spiritual formation journeys of the participants at First Church.

Prayer and discernment became much more of the norm around First Church. At a basic level these activities were an indication that the leaders were recognizing their dependence on the triune God rather than relying only on their insights and abilities. Working through the missional literature reinforced the integral role of spiritual formation for the leaders at First Church. Out of one of the newer books they were reading the idea for a missional discipleship matrix emerged.

In their helpful work, *The Missional Church in Perspective: Mapping Trends and Shaping Conversation*, Van Gelder and Zscheile offer a six-movement argument for the missional church. The leaders at First Church decided to use these arguments to help them understand their context. Those arguments are as follows:

1. The church in North America is now located within a dramatically changed context.
2. The good news of the gospel announced by Jesus as the reign (kingdom) of God needs to shape the identity of the missional church.
3. The missional church with its identity rooted in the reign (kingdom) of God must live as an alternative community in the world.
4. The missional church needs to understand that the Holy Spirit cultivates communities that represent the reign (kingdom) of God.
5. The missional church is to be led by missional leadership that focuses on equipping all of God's people for mission.
6. The missional church needs to develop missional structures for shaping its life and ministry as well as practice missional connectedness with the larger church (Van Gelder and Zscheile, 2011).

These six arguments provided an organizing structure for what they called a missional discipleship matrix. A more generic term might be a comprehensive curriculum. After much discussion, and a few false starts, this convicted group of leaders at First Church came up with a way to flesh out their matrix with codependent experiences of formation and engagement.

The team decided to use the five qualities of missional leadership Pastor Smith had introduced to organize the formation experience: resurrection confidence, robust spirituality, global perspective, heightened curiosity, and a deep love for the church. These qualities had proven to be helpful and were needed by both clergy and laity if the congregation was going to make this transition. Their thinking can be illustrated as follows: *Since the church in North America (read First Church) is now located within a dramatically changed context, how can exercising these qualities of missional leadership help us live into that context? How does (insert missional leadership trait) help us embrace where we find ourselves? What are some ways we can strengthen this quality? What are some things we may need to stop doing in order to strengthen this quality?*

Pastor Smith agreed to preach a series of sermons on each of these qualities. A time of discussion was scheduled to introduce these qualities and their possible implications to the congregation. (One of the pastors interviewed around these qualities, Jack Glasgow, developed a series of five sermons around these leadership qualities. He also conducted discussion sessions with his congregation. Those sermons and discussion guides can be found as an appendix to this book).

A process began to take shape after many discussions, e-mails, and prayers. A congregational discernment process would begin with Pastor Smith's sermon series and discussions focusing on the five qualities of missional leadership. A significant issue emerged over scheduling these discussion sessions. The longtime members assumed this discussion time would be on Wednesday evenings. Many others said they just could not or would not come back downtown for an evening meeting. Another ending was surfacing. Sunday and Wednesday had been the twin towers of program life for First Church for as long as anyone could remember. While no one was advocating eliminating events on these days, their exclusive hold had been broken. A compromise schedule of Sunday lunch and discussion after worship was planned.

This experience turned out positively. Pastor Smith had to get out of his lectionary-text comfort zone to prepare this sermon series. The congregation had to buy in to listening in a way that would allow them to discuss the subject with others.

The leaders discovered that more folk than they expected participated. They also learned that providing child care and children's activities was essential for young adults to be involved. The leadership team was pleased to see more multigenerational interaction than any of them could ever recall.

This experience proved to be informative as the leadership team planned the next phase of their process. The Sunday lunchtime had proven to be effective in terms of both participation and energy. The direct connection with worship seemed to be a factor, but they were not as clear about that as they were the meeting time. The team met for prayer and discernment. They had come to believe that if they were truly pursuing their role in God's mission, God's Spirit would be available to them.

A series of six Sundays was scheduled to explore the movement argument statements (listed on page 85), with one statement as the focus for each Sunday discussion. Pastor Smith and the worship team agreed to allow the statement to influence worship. This could be through a sermon focus, a testimony, or some other worship feature. At the conclusion of worship, an invitation to deeper discussion would be offered.

Following lunch, discussion facilitators would lead small group discussions around tables. The following is an example of the outline for a session:

Statement: *The church in North America is now located within a dramatically changed context.*
   1. Ask the group to list examples of this changed context. Record responses on poster paper.

2. Ask the group to identify some of the implications for First Church that result from these changes. Record responses.
3. Hear brief reports from all small groups.
4. Then ask participants to identify specific potential implications for them personally. Record responses.
5. Offer a time for prayer and reflection in each group.
6. Bring the large group together and ask, "If we take this statement seriously, what difference will it make?"
7. Distribute copies of the "Qualities of Missional Leadership Description Sheet" (created from chapter 4) and ask how these qualities might be helpful for the congregation and for individuals as they face these implications.

This discussion process will be used for each of the six statements over six consecutive weeks. The regular Wednesday evening prayer time would also include opportunities to pray for this process, for each particular focus, and for the individuals in the church and the community.

During the week after each Sunday session, the leadership team will meet to review the process and see what patterns might be emerging from the discussions.

The final piece of this matrix is engagement. After each of the six arguments for the missional church are explored, the congregation must then answer the three missional framing questions:

1. Where are we being called to connect with God's mission at this unique place and time?
2. What do we need to be and do in order to put ourselves in the best position to participate in God's mission?
3. How do we offer the invitation to the congregation, to individuals, and to ourselves as leaders to claim our calling to be the people of God in the world?

After the six discussion sessions have been concluded, a final session will be scheduled. This session will provide for the ultimate "so what" conversation using these three framing missional questions as a guide for their discussion.

In the meantime Pastor Smith shared this process with his peer group, and a new idea emerged. Several pastors wanted to get their congregations into this discussion as well. The peer group tossed the idea around and finally decided that it would be helpful if several congregations could participate in this process and then get together and share their experiences.

Seven congregations agreed to participate in the learning/discernment/application process. After all had concluded the process, members would be invited to join together at First Church on a Saturday morning to share and debrief their experiences. The folk at First Church were surprised and encouraged that other congregations were also focusing on these issues and asking many of the same questions.

This process and these discussions with other churches would guide the leaders of First Church as they worked toward a comprehensive curriculum for spiritual formation and missional engagement. The three framing missional questions would serve as the evaluative questions for the curriculum plan that emerged from this process.

For each of these questions the leader would ask, "What do we need to know, to be, and to do in order to respond to God's invitation?" Bible study, spiritual formation, worship and missional engagement could then find a new relevance and purpose for the folk at First Church.

REFLECTING ON YOUR CONTEXT

Toward Missional

What are some missional actions currently going on in your congregation?

What are some barriers to your congregation's moving toward being missional?

How do you understand the role of discipleship in your church's transition toward becoming missional?

How would you answer the "so what" questions for your congregation?

CHAPTER 7

What Does a Leader Look Like?

The people at First Church are doing good work. A truly amazing step has been taken. Months of work and energy have gone into the discernment process. Both pastor and people are now at another critical point. Many challenges have been identified through this intentional and intense process. Some members are energized by new perspectives that have emerged in the conversations. Other members are feeling overwhelmed at all the different possibilities facing them.

On one hand, people are asking Pastor Smith why the church isn't implementing changes immediately. Perhaps a larger group is taking comfort in the fact that First Church held similar conversations in the past and nothing really changed.

The congregation first needed to celebrate their initial discernment. Cross-generational conversations had taken place as never before, and new relationships had formed. It's time to celebrate, but more work is needed. Technical leaders might be tempted to rest here in the knowledge that they did something and they don't want to upset folk.

The leaders at First Church were beginning to understand that they could not afford to rest here. They realized they were facing a storm of changes and transitions that could shake their beloved church to its foundation. Pastor Smith and the leadership team are now being called to practice a new kind of leadership. They are being called to lead in a new way.

Being an adaptive leader and working through these transitions can put a strain on relationships. As we have stated earlier, the pastor must have a deep love for the church and its people to offer effective leadership through the transition process. He or she must demonstrate that love in an ongoing, consistent way. The people need to know that they are loved in a way that sustains them as they face numerous transitions and adaptive challenges. The missional journey and its necessary transitions are a highly relational venture. A deep level of trust is going to be necessary to face the transitional challenges ahead.

Many congregational leaders have discovered that one of the keys to breaking the Christendom patterns of operating and therefore refocusing on relationships is revisiting one's call, one's vocation. Returning to God's call on our life brings us to a place of vulnerability, honesty, and intimacy with self and God. Pastor Smith's questions led him to just such a place. God's call for him grew out of his being loved by his family and his church family. It was informed by his understanding of Scripture and seeing what God's call looked like in others. It was first an intimate relationship with God, not the first step in a career path. He began to realize that, over the years, his ability to listen for God had been drowned out by the noise of the institution. Pastor Smith knew that he wanted and needed to reembrace his vocation. He knew he wanted to be the type of leader his congregation needed more than what they wanted. Now was his "so what" time.

This was not a quick process for Bill Smith. The unanswerable questions kept pushing him to look for answers. Bill finally began to share at a more intimate level with fellow pastors in his peer group. To his amazement most of them were struggling with similar questions. As they shared stories, their discussions became more focused and more urgent. Bill confided that their missional discussions had focused the disconnect he was feeling between his call and his work as a pastor. Practically every other pastor in the group said "amen!" As their discussion continued, they shared resources they had found helpful or thought might be helpful to others. The conversation eventually focused on their individual need for a deeper, more meaningful spiritual life. They began by planning a retreat to create space to focus on their intimate relationship with God. Bill had let his daily busyness keep him from giving time to his own spiritual life. He realized that if he was going to stay true to his calling, he had to transition from neglecting his spiritual life to investing time in a more robust spirituality. Bill carved out time each day for Scripture reading and reflection that was not directly related to sermons, funerals, prayer meetings, or wedding preparation. As he began to be fed by this experience, Bill worked to protect and guard this time in his daily schedule.

Bill's peer group continued to be a vital part of the encouragement he needed to do the hard work of being an adaptive leader. As they continued to discuss the works of Heifetz, Roxburgh, and others, Bill began to see ways to address his frustration over the disconnect between his call and his role as pastor of First Church. Bill's peer group provided a safe place to ask questions, to share frustrations and fears, and to float new and potentially risky ideas.

One particular peer group meeting seemed to be an "aha moment" for many participants. They were discussing an early article by Heifetz and Laurie that introduced the basics of adaptive leadership (Heifetz and Laurie, 1997). In this article the authors state that adaptive leadership is needed "when our deeply held beliefs are challenged, when the values that made us successful become less relevant, and when legitimate yet competing perspectives emerge." This group of pastors agreed that this was exactly the situation they and their congregations were facing. They were dealing with all three of these challenges at once. There seemed to be a sense of relief that their situation had been diagnosed. But as the discussion continued, the group began to realize the magnitude of the difficult challenge before them.

Their congregations, for the most part, were not prepared for the tasks ahead. These churches had a long history of providing a technical fix and moving on. If, after a time, the pastor could not come up with the proper fix, the church would look for a new pastor with what they perceived to be just the right gadgets in his or her toolbox to solve their problem. These pastors knew that if they pushed too hard or too fast, they would put their jobs in jeopardy and the churches' effectiveness at risk. The group continued to meet and share stories of how they were trying to lead in a different way in their congregations.

As Bill Smith continued to read and participate in discussions focused on a number of resources, he was confronted with one clear issue: Whatever the challenge, the responsibility for addressing that challenge belongs to the people in the congregation and could not be assigned to just the pastor and staff.

Bill had played basketball in high school and college, and he still tried to get on the court a couple of times a week. As he was confronted with a new way of thinking about his role as pastor/leader, he saw a parallel with the function of his coaches. They did all they could to prepare the players. Ultimately the coach's goal was to prepare the team to focus completely on winning the next game. The bottom line was winning the game. The coach tried to create an environment that would bring out the best in each player, whether he was a starter or a reserve.

Being a pastor trying to lead a congregation to deal with adaptive challenges had several similarities to Bill's coaches. As pastor, Bill needed to help the congregation focus on the challenges. When they got distracted by lesser issues, the pastor had to call them back to focus. He had to help create an environment where church members responded out of their understanding of being called to be the people of God in the world. The pastor had to help focus the congregation on its bottom line—thriving as the people of God at this unique place and time. Like his coach the pastor had to let the people do the work of making the transitions they were facing. His basketball coach could not play the game for him. Bill could not make the transition for his church.

Slowly Bill's outlook began to change. He began to understand that he had to take off the heavy traditional role of pastor, as he had come to understand it, and lay it down. Through continuing conversations with fellow pastors, Bill was confronted with one of his operating assumptions. He had allowed the congregation to place responsibility for its success in his hands as pastor. The authority and the great sense of being needed were a tempting recipe for failure. Bill began to realize what was happening. Both he and the congregation were putting their confidence in their ability to fix their situation and, if you pushed them, to fix the world's problems as well!

As Bill continued to be intentional about his own spiritual journey, he began to realize that this confidence was misplaced. *If my calling is to be about God's mission, then my confidence must reside in God and God's faithfulness to God's mission*, Bill began to understand. Our confidence must be found in the resurrected Christ and in Christ's invitation to us to accept and enter God's kingdom. Our confidence in a sending God gives us the courage to live in and invite others into the shalom space that is God's kingdom. The strategy was not to think about the church less and the kingdom more. That approach is an invitation for church members to disconnect. Many find it difficult to connect to some esoteric idea. Pastor Smith began to realize that a more effective strategy would be to create an environment in which members of the church and community could begin to understand the church in light of God's kingdom. Pastor Smith was beginning to see God's mission as the link between the church and the kingdom. This perspective offers the possibility of increased energy and clarity of purpose and meaning.

Bill's calling from God was not to be a technician fixing whatever problem came along from person or program. He had been and was being called to participate in God's mission in the world.

He had a particular calling to pastor the people of God to be about God's mission of reconciling the world. Bill began to imagine the possibilities. *What is God calling us to be and do in the world?* Bill wondered. *How can we free ourselves up to be open to and curious about what God is doing in the world? What would it look like if First Church began to connect with God's mission in new and exciting ways?* Bill found himself filled with questions that he was interested in engaging the congregation to discover the answers.

As Bill began to reembrace his vocation, he was able to see First Church and his role as pastor in a different light. He was able to put on the role of pastor again, but he understood that role in a new way. This role seemed to fit more comfortably. He could be Pastor Smith again. But helping the congregation understand his new role and his newly forming perspective would take both time and intentionality.

At this point Pastor Smith began conversations with the leadership team that led to the sermon series on the Qualities of Missional Leaders and the congregational discernment process.

Pastor Smith now came to understand even more clearly that if he was to respond effectively to God's call, he had to invest himself with the people of First Church and its community. Practically, that meant that his default response was "no" when other churches began to show interest in his moving and becoming their pastor. Pastor Smith began to realize that he believed in God's mission and that he believed in the people at First Church, and he was excited about their journey together. Pastor Smith began appreciatively to anticipate the task ahead. He had the luxury of a theological education. He was expected to be "spiritual." He was supposed to understand the Bible and be the resident expert on God. Even with all that, Pastor Smith had a difficult time getting to this new place of missional understanding. Obviously it was going to take a lot of time, trust, and growth together for First Church and its leaders to come to this new perspective of what it means to be the people of God in the world today.

Worship Woes

The congregational discernment process identified several places where deeply held beliefs were being challenged. Some values that had made them successful seemed less relevant, and competing perspectives emerged. Also, to no one's surprise, competing responses to these challenges also emerged.

Having people become engaged with exploring what it means to connect with God's mission does not mean that problems in a congregation are over. The life of a congregation is complex with multiple issues pressing for attention at the same time.

Unfortunately, people who seem to "get it" when it comes to working with refugee families may "miss it" altogether in some other area. First Church continued to have challenges. The background noise was getting louder. One of the most emotionally charged adaptive challenges that was named in the discernment process was worship. More and more individuals and groups were expressing concern over the reality of declining worship attendance. In the past Pastor Smith would carry this burden as his personal responsibility. He would work to preach "better" sermons. Yet he knew from his years of preaching that *better* had a wide range of meanings. A variety of technical fixes had been suggested: "Maybe we should change our Sunday schedule to accommodate those who want to get through early." "We should have a wider variety of music than our traditional fare." "Drums are the answer! All the growing churches use drums." "Perhaps we need to have two worship venues on Sunday morning." "Why don't we let the young folk have their loud music on Sunday night?" Still another suggested: "We need to renovate our sanctuary. Some fresh paint and new carpet will make it more attractive to newcomers." It seems that everyone has a suggestion on how to "fix" a problem.

Often the point of leadership paralysis in a congregation is the belief that you have to have the ultimate and safe answer to the problem before you can or should do anything. Pastor Smith had been encouraged by his peer group discussions around adaptive leadership. He realized the tensions and expectations that had been raised around worship could no longer be ignored.

Because he was trying a new approach to an old and difficult problem, Pastor Smith took great care to follow the steps of the adaptive leadership process. He reviewed the steps in this process with the leadership team, and they used the steps to guide them through the swamp of tradition, emotion, threat, fear, and heightened anxiety they were wading into. What follows is a snapshot of some of the basic issues and questions these steps helped the team clarify.

Get on the Balcony

Worship and the Sunday schedule had been recurring issues as First Church members struggled with the "so what" questions during their discernment process. Pastor Smith and the leadership team decided these issues could not wait.

The leaders knew they had to get the big-picture view of what was going on here. They needed to "get on the balcony" to grasp the dynamics of this situation. An overnight retreat was planned for the team, and the music and worship committee was invited to participate.

Retreat participants were asked to reflect on the meaning of worship in their lives. They were asked to recall especially meaningful worship experiences and to get in touch with why they were so meaningful. After a time of sharing, the group realized that worship had been meaningful for a variety of reasons at many different points along their journeys. From this more collaborative balcony view, they began to identify the specific adaptive challenge First Church was facing.

Identify the Challenge

As the conversation unfolded, one of the music and worship committee members observed: "I think we have been starting at the wrong place. I know I have. When we talk about worship, I have always started from *how* we worship, but our conversation has helped me see that I need to begin with *why* we worship." Silence followed for a minute. Then one by one all agreed with this new insight. After much conversation back and forth, the group realized at least a tentative agreement on the fundamental challenge. It is not, "How do we accommodate everyone's taste in worship?" but rather: "How do we articulate why we worship in the first place, and how does this understanding move us closer to embracing our role in God's kingdom? What role does and should worship play in our missional journey?"

Regulate Distress

The group knew that the congregation as a whole had not had this retreat experience. Pastor Smith was keenly aware that even some of the retreat participants were anxious about where this discussion might lead. The group named this issue and began to focus on how to address it.

Again, after much discussion, the group agreed on a plan. They decided to schedule a time in each adult and youth Bible study group to invite them to a similar conversation about their experiences

The fact that worship kept coming up in the discernment discussions was no secret. Anxiety was up throughout the congregation. The challenge was to acknowledge this issue and to find healthy ways to address it. A growing group of leaders was beginning to understand that if the congregation was going to address the adaptive challenge of the role of worship in moving them toward embracing their role in God's mission, they had to lean into the distress rather than try to ignore it or eliminate it.

Maintain Disciplined Attention

Given the nature of congregational life, this step in the adaptive leadership process may prove to be the most challenging. Congregational leaders do not have the luxury of focusing on one issue until it is resolved. Pastor Smith and the leadership team at First Church had to continue to focus on the role of worship while at the same time dealing with budget promotion, pastoral care crises, study and worship preparation, and day-to-day operations.

To keep this issue from falling victim to any one person's distraction, the group who had been on the retreat together agreed to check-in meetings every two weeks. These were brief, stand-up meetings after worship to make sure the conversation was continuing in the congregation. These meetings also helped them identify next steps the process needed to take.

Give the Work Back to the People

This step can also be a challenge. Many church members have been trained to let the pastor and staff do the work. Particularly with a challenging issue, many church members would rather not have it given back to them. After Bible study conversations and seemingly endless informal discussions, the normal practice at First Church had been to charge a committee to craft a recommendation for the church to vote up or down. The leaders knew that would not be an adequate approach when members' values, beliefs, and behaviors were being challenged.

A town hall meeting was scheduled to invite the congregation to own this issue. The leadership team was nervous about how this meeting would go, but they were convinced that any decision made would not work if it was imposed, even by a majority vote.

To no one's surprise, after two hours of conversation the group was not ready for resolution. Another town hall meeting was scheduled, and after the third such meeting some clarity and consensus began to emerge.

Protect Voices of Leadership from Below

The pastor and the leadership team were acutely aware that a number of people would not participate in the town hall discussions. Regardless of how rich and meaningful the discussion, those who were not heard needed to know they are valued and their perspectives are important.

One group the pastor identified was the youth. They had been included in the Bible study discussions and were invited to the town hall conversations. As expected, however, they did not choose to participate in these meeting with many of their parents and grandparents. The leadership team arranged to have a time to discuss worship with the entire youth group during one of their regularly scheduled Sunday evening gatherings. Their perspectives were added to those already heard.

A second, less obvious group, included regular worshippers who were not official members of First Church. Some people regularly attended worship but were not involved in other activities. The team wanted to include their perspectives as well. They heard the announcements about the town hall meetings, but because they were not official members, they did not feel free to participate in those discussions.

Team members each took three of these individuals or couples and contacted them personally. They arranged a time to meet with them individually to hear their perspective and to make sure they knew they were valued.

• • •

It has become obvious by now that I am not offering specific insights or details that surfaced during this process. Neither am I suggesting specific solutions. That is not the point of this work. This is not intended to be an owner's manual for a happy church. Your congregation is unique. The role you discover to play as the people of God in the world grows out of the congregation's self-awareness of its unique identity. The people in your congregation have never been at this specific point on their individual spiritual journeys. Your community has never presented such an array of spiritual needs and challenges to your congregation.

I am convinced congregational leaders need to understand the difference between change and transition. We need tools to assist us as we lead our congregations to thrive in the midst of these epochal transitions. We need to understand that the familiar technical solutions may allow us to survive but not to thrive in this environment.

Along with some specific tools, we have discussed the fact that congregational leadership is personal and highly relational. Five specific qualities that contribute to effective congregational leadership when exercised over time have been presented and briefly illustrated.

I hope that you now have a clearer sense of the time of great transition we are experiencing. And I hope that the resources reviewed in this book will give you some handles for thriving in the midst of constant change.

I have used the image of the bottom line at several points along the way. We need to conclude with what for me is the ultimate bottom line: "For God so loved the world that he gave his only Son, so that everyone who believes in him may not perish but may have eternal life" (John 3:16).

The world, our neighbors, our church members, and our families need to know that God loves them. How are they going to know unless we as the people of God show them?

REFLECTING ON YOUR CONTEXT

Putting Leadership into Practice

What are the three most pressing adaptive challenges your congregation is facing?

Choose one of your adaptive challenges and list ways the various elements of adaptive leadership listed below could be helpful.
Get on the balcony.
Identify the adaptive challenge.
Regulate the distress.
Maintain attention on the challenge.
Give work back to the people.
Protect voices from below.

Five Qualities of Missional Leadership

How can you see the leadership qualities listed below being exercised in your congregation?
Resurrection Confidence
Robust Spirituality
Heightened Sense of Curiosity
Global Perspective
Deep Love for the Church

BIBLIOGRAPHY

Barna, George. *Revolution.* Carol Stream, IL: Barna Books, 2005.

Bosch, David. *Transforming Mission: Paradigm Shifts in Theology of Mission.* Maryknoll, NY: Orbis Books, 1991.

Bridges, William. *Transitions: Making Sense of Life's Changes.* Cambridge, MA: DeCapo Press, 2004.

Drucker, Peter F. *Post-Capitalist Society.* New York: HarperBusiness, 1993.

Guder, Darrell L. *Missional Church: A Vision for the Sending of the Church in North America.* Grand Rapids: Eerdmans, 1998.

Heifetz, Ronald A. *Leadership without Easy Answers.* Boston: Harvard University Press, 1994.

Heifetz, Ronald A., Alexander Grashow, and Marty Linsky. *The Practice of Adaptive Leadership.* Boston: Harvard Business School Press, 2009.

Heifetz, Ronald A., and Donald L. Laurie. "The Work of Leadership." *Harvard Business Review.* January-February 1997.

Heifetz, Ronald A. and Marty Linsky. *Leadership on the Line.* Boston: Harvard Business School Press, 2002.

Mulholland, M. Robert, Jr. *Invitation to a Journey: A Road Map for Spiritual Formation.* Nottingham, UK: IVP Books, 1993.

Roxburgh, Alan J. and Fred Romanuk. *The Missional Leader: Equipping Your Church to Reach a Changed World.* San Francisco: Jossey-Bass, 2006.

Tickle, Phillis. *The Great Emergence: How Christianity is Changing and Why.* Grand Rapids: Baker Books, 2008.

Van Gelder, Craig, and Dwight J. Zscheile, *The Missional Church in Perspective: Mapping Trends and Shaping the Conversation.* Grand Rapids: Baker Academic, 2011.

Wright, N. T. *Surprised by Hope: Rethinking Heaven, the Resurrection, and the Mission of the Church.* New York: HarperOne, 2008.

APPENDIX

Sermons for Churches in Transition

Jack Glasgow, pastor of Zebulon Baptist Church in Zebulon, North Carolina, preached a series of sermons on the five qualities of missional leadership. He has graciously offered to share both the sermon texts and his congregational discussion guides.

Resurrection Confidence
1 Corinthians 15:12-22, 50-58

If the church is to be truly missional in the twenty-first century, it will need far more than missional leaders among its pastors,. It will need you to rise up and become great missional leaders—deacons, Sunday school teachers, mission volunteers, youth and children's ministry volunteers, ministry team leaders. It is time to raise up a generation of church members who want so much more than to be passive members and participants in the church; they must want to be authentic followers of Jesus, who like the first generation of disciples, embraced the missional lifestyle and made a difference in the world for the cause of Christ.

If members of the clergy need to embrace and embody certain qualities in the missional church movement, laity need to embrace and embody those same qualities; for laypersons will be the most consequential leaders in the church's carrying out God's mission in the world with faithfulness to Jesus in the power of the Holy Spirit. Simply put, you need to know about these five qualities.

The first quality exhibited by a missional leader is *resurrection confidence*. Jesus is alive. Christ is risen, He is risen indeed. Jesus is set loose. The tomb is empty. The living Jesus is now our living Lord.

Terry Hamrick spoke of resurrection confidence for missional leaders: "Such ministers live out their vocational lives with a vibrant sense that Christ is alive, present, and working in the congregation and the world. When a minister's preaching, teaching, worship leadership, and care for the congregation are informed primarily by the reality of resurrection, real joy is present. When the empty tomb dictates our vision, captures our imagination, focuses our discernment, and empowers our relationships in the congregation and the community, the ministry is marked by a sure and certain hope."

This applies to all of us in the church. Nothing will make a greater difference in the vibrancy and attractiveness of our Christian life than our confidence in the resurrection. We can all carry out tasks in the church and do good deeds in the world. But those actions are powerfully transformed when done with great confidence in the resurrection. This is indeed the source of our joy and the stimulus for our imagination and creativity in serving Christ. We must want so much more than just to go through the motions of church and ministry. As we do what the old hymn says and "serve a risen Savior who is in the world today," the ministry of all Christians becomes marked by great hope and renewed power.

Paul underscores the importance of resurrection confidence most emphatically in 1 Corinthians 15. Those poor Corinthians certainly made a bundle of mistakes that opened them up for Paul's stinging critiques. Undoubtedly, some among them were saying, "There is no resurrection from the dead," denying what Paul had emphasized as being of first importance to the Corinthians when he preached the gospel to them, "that Christ died for our sins in accordance with the scriptures, and that he was buried, and that he was raised on the third day in accordance with the Scriptures" (vv. 3–4).

Some within the tattered fellowship of the believers at Corinth had given up their hope in resurrection. It was just too hard to believe. Miracles are hard for the intellectual to accept. They were not arguing to give up on the teachings of Jesus and trying to be a faith community together; they just wanted to do it apart from the belief in resurrection. But Paul would have no part of this. He did not mix words. If there is no resurrection, our preaching is in vain. If we can't believe in our own resurrection in Christ, then how can we believe in Christ's own resurrection? Our faith is in vain. We are preaching a gospel of falsehood. Our faith is worthless. We are still in our sins. The dead in Christ simply perish. If we are basing our faith and hope only in the earthly life of Jesus, and can't embrace with faith his resurrection, then we are fools to be pitied.

Has Paul lost his confidence in the resurrection? Not at all. Christ has been raised from the dead, the firstfruits of all who will be raised in Christ. By man came death. The first man, Adam, died, and all who follow after him will die. The second man, Jesus, died and rose again. And in Christ all shall be made alive. In Christ God has conquered not just sin but also death. I can hear the choir sing the mournful notes from Handel's *Messiah*: "Since by man came death." Then I hear them burst into joyful song, "Even so in Christ, shall all be made alive."

At the end of the chapter, Paul wants to assure the Corinthian Christians that they too, shall be raised with Christ. We die, and our bodies are sown as a seed sown into the ground, in the hope of being raised to newness of life, transferred from the realm of the perishable into life that never fades or perishes. Is Paul making sense here, explaining the resurrection like a logical apologist? No, Paul understood his hope in the resurrection was a faith claim. He called it all by the name, great mystery. But Paul embraced the mystery with unwavering faith and claimed the great victory of the resurrection in Christ Jesus.

Such confidence fuels the passion and mission of the church. Through meeting the risen Christ on the Damascus road, Paul was forever changed. He makes the case for why resurrection confidence is essential to missional following of Jesus. The last verse of this great chapter tells us why resurrection confidence is so important: "Therefore, my beloved, be steadfast, immovable, always excelling in the work of the Lord, because you know that in the Lord your labor is not in vain."

A steadfast congregation of believers who abound in the work of the Lord in the world with confidence that their labor will make a difference will be fueled by their own confidence in the resurrection of Jesus. A great challenge for us who desire to be on mission, who want to get out and serve others, is for us to admit the importance of resurrection confidence. It is tempting in our twenty-first-century realism to abandon mystery and simply remember the teachings of Jesus and get out there and heal and love and serve others like Jesus did, with lessened emphasis on the story of death, burial, and resurrection. We can easily be misled that the evangelism of good deeds is far more effective than the evangelism of proclaiming the gospel. Those who focus on good works, with little thought given to resurrection, can easily fall into the practice of exalting ourselves for our Christian activism and feeling superior to Christians who seem to need the crutch of talking so much about resurrection and heaven and everlasting life. We need to be honest about our faith and about our Scriptures and understand that by embracing the great mystery we will find the passion and power and energy to make our mission in the world an amazing work of God through us as opposed to a work we do in human strength for God's sake or in memory of Jesus.

Sadly we have given resurrection confidence one Sunday on the calendar as opposed to a central place in our confessional theology. On Easter we break out of our Lenten and Holy Week focus on confession and suffering and sing with gusto, "The strife is o'er." "Christ the Lord is risen today." "Christ is alive, let Christians sing." "Up from the grave he arose." And "He lives!" Yet every Sunday is to be a celebration of the resurrection. Every day of a Christian's life needs to be lived in joyful confidence that "Christ is alive." Such resurrection confidence is crucial to the church's producing Christians who are steadfast and immovable, abounding in the work of the Lord in the confidence that their labor is not in vain because Christ is alive!

It was close to Easter 1990. Having my lost my dad to cancer in 1982 at the age of 53, now my 59-year-old mother was in the late stages of metastatic renal cell carcinoma. She had been living with us, and now we were on our way to the hospital. Soon she would be admitted for a three-and-a-half-month hospital stay that would end in her death on July 31, 1990. On the way to see her radiologist that day, Mom spoke to me in a serious tone. She said: "You are my son and now you are my pastor. I know I don't have long. I have faith that I will go to heaven, but my faith is not completely free of doubt. You have studied and you have preached many funerals. I want to know, do you really think your dad is alive today with God? Do you really think I will be?"

If ever a minister's resurrection confidence was on the line, it was then. This was no time for a preacher's pat answer. The woman who carried me and brought me into this world and nurtured me was on her way out, and she wanted to know, did I really believe she would continue to be raised to new life?

I remember telling Mother that I could not prove it to her, I could not explain it, because the resurrection is a great and wonderful mystery. But, yes, down deep within me, I believe in the resurrection. When I preach funerals for the beloved members of our church and I tell their families about the resurrection, I am not just trying to make them feel better. I really do believe. I told her I had my own doubts and questions, and I frankly did not see that as a spiritual weakness or problem. But, yes, I do believe. I put in a cassette and played a song I truly love, "Calvary's Love." We both listened to the wonderful words, "Souls still take eternal passage, sins atoned, and heaven gained."

She learned to love that song. It fed her own resurrection confidence, and in those final months she was a marvelous witness for Christ. Nurses grew to love her, and after shifts some would sit by her bedside and tell her about some of their own problems, and she would pray with them. She was a missional Christian from her dying bed. Her Jewish oncologist joked with me, "If your Mother does not hurry up and die, she will have all of us converted." I could not have been prouder. I knew that her end of life spurt as a missional Christian had been fed by her confidence in the great mystery of the resurrection.

This morning, whatever your life situation, God is calling you to work and ministry and witness. God has a role for you in God's mission in this world. At home, at school, in church, in your neighborhood, in your work, in your travel, God calls you to be on mission. Where will you find your energy for such a high calling? Where will you find the strength? Where will you find the passion? Where will you find the gifts you need for such a mission?

Let me suggest a great place to start. Jesus is alive. Believe it. Against all odds, with amazing mystery and wonder, God has raised Jesus from the tomb. He is loosed from the graveclothes and set free. That ought to make you happy. That ought to bring you deep joy. That ought to help you believe that with God all things are possible. As you ponder this deep mystery of grace, it ought to bring you abiding, deep peace. Be confident in Christ's resurrection; it is the way to that steadfast Christian life that always abounds in God's work.

SERMON DISCUSSION QUESTIONS
RESURRECTION CONFIDENCE

1. What stood out in the sermon that you would like to discuss?

2. How hard is it to have resurrection confidence? What are the greatest barriers?

3. How can one practice resurrection confidence without turning faith in the resurrection into some propositional truth that one must believe without any doubts?

4. What does it mean to embrace the resurrection as mystery?

5. What hymns and Bible verses come to mind that speak to you of resurrection confidence?

6. How does one practice resurrection confidence without coming across too preachy? Without coming across that their perception of the risen Christ is the right perception?

7. How do you think resurrection confidence translates practically into missional Christianity and missional leadership? Why do you think such confidence is essential for the missional Christian?

8. Who is a good example that comes to mind of resurrection confidence? Do you see that person as a missional Christian? A missional leader? How does their resurrection confidence impact their Christian life and witness?

Robust Spirituality
Ephesians 1:3-19a

Robust. Now that's a wonderful, rich, expressive word. "Strong," "healthy," "vigorous," "rich and full"—these are some of the words Merriam-Webster uses to define *robust*. It is from the Latin root *robur*, which means "oak," as in the majestic oak tree. To be robust is to be big and large and strong and majestic like the oak.

As we are focusing on five qualities of missional Christian leaders, this morning we take a look at the second of those five qualities: "robust spirituality." Here is what Terry Hamrick has written about the robust spirituality demonstrated by pastors who are missional leaders: "Among these ministers is an obvious and growing personal faith, marked by prayer, study, and commitment to spiritual disciplines. Congregants recognize that their minister's life is marked by a vibrant faith, a deeply committed relationship to the risen Christ, and they are drawn into that same kind of relationship."

What Terry says about clergy who are missional leaders holds true for men and women and youth who will be Christian missional leaders. They will have a growing faith and a deep relationship with God. Their lives are deeply rooted in worship and Bible study, prayer, and Christian fellowship. They will have a joy and vitality that makes their service to the Lord and the church more than dull obedience to the tasks of ministry or prideful arrogance over their work on God's behalf. Persons with a vibrant spiritual life will serve God with joy in such a way that attracts people to Jesus. It is the fulfillment of what Jesus declared when he called those who were listening to him "the light of the world" and "the salt of the earth." He instructed them, "Let your light shine before others, so that they may see your good works and give glory to your Father in heaven" (Matt. 5:16). Mission work done apart from robust spirituality makes little impact. But, flowing from a robust spiritual life, persons engaged in mission change things/ They change others and they change circumstances.

We live in a beautiful part of the world. Oak trees abound, providing abundant shade to lawns and avenues. We all lament when we lose a grand oak to the winds of hurricanes, tornadoes, or storms, to old age and disease, or especially to "progress" in the form of development that requires the removal of a majestic oak tree. Robust, like an oak tree; that's a powerful image.

In the text from Ephesians 1, the apostle Paul is writing in a form that resembles a hymn. After greeting the Christians at Ephesus, he writes in lyrical fashion as in a hymn. Paul wants the believers there to know just how much they have been given in Christ—spiritual blessings, redemption, forgiveness, a marvelous inheritance, the seal of the Holy Spirit. The chorus of his hymn would be, "To the praise of His glory," an oft-repeated phrase that explains we have been given great gifts in Christ that we might live our lives to the praise of God's glory. Paul finishes the hymn by offering a prayer that they would have the eyes of their hearts opened to see God's great hope when he called them to faith in Jesus, to see the great riches of God's inheritance given to them in Christ, and to recognize the surpassing greatness of God's power extended to all who believe in the Lord.

The danger of any hymn is that people may find it easy to read or sing, even with gusto, but pay little attention to its message. I don't want us to make that mistake with this great hymn from Ephesians. The message of this beautiful text is this: God has given us the gift of himself in Christ. The gift is rich and wonderful, powerful and amazing. In Jesus we have been given so much, a relationship with God that heals our lives and strengthens our spirits and encourages our hearts. We can ignore the gift and barely enjoy its richness and fullness. How many of us have useful gifts at home that we fail to use to the fullest—exercise equipment, cookware, and various gadgets we received as gifts but have relegated to closet and pantry shelves? We can, however, take the time and make the effort to enjoy the gift to the fullest. When we make that choice to enjoy all the gifts of God, our spirits soar. We worship God and read the Bible and pray, all in the enjoyment of a warm, spiritual community of believers. Our lives are changed and strengthened. Like the oak. Like what Psalm 1 describes as "trees planted by streams of water, which yield their fruit in its season." In a word, we become by God's great grace "robust."

A robust spiritual life. How well does that describe you today? How did you answer the last time someone asked you how you were doing? Stressed, busy, tired, worn out—so many of us use these descriptive words if we think someone really cares to know how we feel. If not, we probably use words like *fine*, *good*, or *well* to answer the question and just keep on our not so merry way. Wouldn't it be great if someone said of us, "No need to ask how you are doing because I can tell by your robust spirit that you are doing great!"

One of the great failings of the church today is that we keep asking tired, worn-out, overcommitted, dull, empty, and/or lifeless people to get busy for the Lord. Teach the class, find a ministry, go to the mission field, serve as a deacon, lead the mission group—it might even perk up your listless spirit. That is why we have become churches filled with people who only commit to short-term assignments or mission experiences. You can sort of "fake it" or pump yourself up for a day of mission service or a weekend of ministry or to be a substitute called on occasionally. But to commit to a lifestyle of mission service, to say yes to a calling to teach, or serve, or minister for the long haul simply will not work if our spiritual lives are anemic. And so, the twenty-first-century church finds itself filled with the burned out, those running on fumes, and those who can only sprint short distances when it comes to serving God.

If we are going to get missional Christianity right, we will have to begin with an invitation to the abundant life of following Jesus. We will have to remind people of all that is ours "in Christ" and demonstrate to them the wonderful difference it makes to be filled with the Spirit of God. We must find joy in the spiritual disciplines of the church and offer them openly and attractively to the spiritually undernourished people of our communities and congregations. It is time to develop robust Christian spirits in our churches, spiritual oaks, and initiate others into the ways of growing spiritually so that they too find their way to robustness in Christ.

If the church decides its attention must be on mission instead of developing robust spiritual lives, we will get it all wrong. We must understand the relationship of a robust spirit to a life of great service. Only when we enjoy the great gift of Christ and are filled with all of the good things we have "in Him" are we ready to live a life that is to the praise of the glory of God.

My friend Jeff Clark, pastor of the First Baptist Church of Sanford, Florida, has always signed his newsletter columns "to the praise of his glory." What an amazing phrase that is, "to the praise of his glory." Even more amazing is to consider what it would really mean to live that way, to be a person of such robust Christian spirit that persons observe your life and praise the glory of God for what they see in you. A life that earns praise for God's glory will always be a balanced Christian life, a balance between spirituality and service, between nurturing one's relationship with Christ and ministering to others in Jesus' name.

I remember the difference in my Christian life in high school and college. In high school I was so busy. My church attendance was limited to about 50 percent on Sunday mornings and occasional Sunday nights. My prayer life was limited, and I read the Bible only occasionally. Yet I still tried to be an active Christian. I was good for an occasional sprint in serving Christ. But my spiritual life didn't have much stamina. My spirit was in no way robust. In fact, it felt pretty empty. I was not the missional Christian leader as a teen that I could have been.

As those of you who have known me are aware, something changed in college. I was still busy. But a new church family was the catalyst for great change in my life. My life was filled, truly filled, with Christian fellowship, a hunger and thirst for worship, a love for the music of the church, and hours spent in Bible study. For the first time I was experiencing all there is to experience "in Christ," and for the first time my spirit was at least approaching that wonderful descriptive word *robust*.

I was not too busy with spiritual things to find time to serve God. A robust spirit developing in me was the energy I needed to find my way to God's mission for my life, to humbly attempt to live a life that might at least approach being lived "to the praise of his glory."

This morning I want you to know that I see great potential in all of you. You can live lives that are fully engaged in serving God in the world. You have the ability to make a difference in you homes and families, in your neighborhood and community, in this church and in the world. You really do. You can live a life to the praise of God's glory. You can be a missional leader. But for your service to be lasting and genuine, you will need great passion and energy. You will need a robust spirit, a spirit that bears the fruits of the Spirit—love and joy, peace and patience, kindness and goodness, faithfulness, gentleness, and self-control. Only ministry done with the fruit of the Spirit will impress persons to see your good works and glorify your Father in heaven. You and I need to invest our lives fully in spiritual practices and disciplines and fellowship to spark our growth in Christ.

A majestic oak tree does so many things. Limbs for playful children to climb. Shade from the sun's summer heat. A pretty decent umbrella in a rain shower. Acorns for the squirrels. Branches for a bird to nest. A sturdy trunk on which tired backs and shoulders can lean. A gorgeous canopy over a small town's main street. Beautiful colors—spring green, deeper summer green, brilliant gold in autumn, snow-covered branches in winter. Even in death, perhaps becoming a piece of solid furniture to last for years to come. All begun by a small acorn taking root in fertile soil and many years of growth.

God has called you to become an oak. It starts with a small seed of faith, but when rightly planted in the fertile soil of God's Spirit, in all of the richness we have in Christ, we grow. We grow to be strong and vibrant, full and vigorous—to be spiritually robust. We become the oak that feeds and protects and nourishes and inspires others. We live out God's mission for our lives—all to the praise of God's glory.

SERMON DISCUSSION QUESTIONS
ROBUST SPIRITUALITY

1. What ideas or thoughts did this sermon generate in your mind?

2. What did the example of the oak tree say to you about robust spirituality?

3. What do you think Paul is trying to communicate through the phrase "to the praise of his glory?

4. In the sermon the point was made that people who spend time nurturing their spiritual life will, surprisingly, be find time for mission and service over the long haul. Why is this true?

5. Undernourished spiritual lives have produced Christians who want to serve and be on mission for short sprints of energy and effort rather than committing to service on an ongoing basis. Why is this so? What can we do to bring about effective change? What cultural factors will we have to contend with to bring about this change?

6. Who are your "heroes" who have robust Christian spirits? Are they also good servants of the Lord? What can you learn from their example?

7. Comment on the idea that the church is depending too much on asking tired and near-empty members to engage in mission in the hopes that it will revive their spirits. How well is this working? How can we change this for the better?

Global Perspective
Acts 11:19-30; 13:1-4

I am always surprised by some of church names. There really are churches with names like Black Jack, Splitwell, and my favorite, Hanging Dog. Even churches with biblical names surprise me. Churches have named themselves after Thessalonica, Corinth, Galatia, Babylon, and Laodicea. Think about it—with all the problems Paul addresses with the Corinthian Christians, why would any church name itself after Corinth? Do a group of Christians with strange and incorrect ideas about the return of Christ decide to name themselves Thessalonica? Laodicea, actually a prominent name among Primitive Baptist churches in years gone by, is a strange choice. That's the church that was neither hot nor cold, that Jesus would just as soon spew from his mouth according to the words to the seven churches in the Revelation of John. Are we sure we want to be associated with that church? And, New Babylon Baptist Church—as they say on Saturday Night Live—"*Really?*"

If I thought a biblical name was a good idea for a local congregation, I would choose Antioch. I don't know anything bad about the church at Antioch. Nothing about the Antioch believers would embarrass a church with that name. The hardest thing for an Antioch Church to do would be live up to the reputation and example of its biblical predecessors.

This morning's sermon takes a look at the third of our five qualities of missional leaders—"global perspective." Christians whose lives inspire and encourage us invariably have a true appreciation for the global perspective of the gospel. Jesus gave believers a commission that is global in scope: Go into all the world and make disciples (see Matt. 28:19). Start where you are with a witness to your Jerusalem and Judea, but understand you are called to be a witness to your Samaria and even the uttermost parts of the earth. The New Testament tells us about a community of believers that took Christ's Commission with the utmost seriousness. They are the first-century church at Antioch, and they serve us well as examples of Christians with a global perspective.

The story of the church at Antioch begins in Acts 11. After the stoning of Stephen, believers scattered in the face of likely persecution. They traveled to Antioch, among other places, and preached the gospel to Jews only. But others traveled to Antioch preaching Jesus to Greeks also. And from the Gentile community many believed the gospel. Their zeal for their newfound faith received attention. The believers in Jerusalem heard of their faith, and Barnabas came to encourage and teach them. He sent for Paul in nearby Tarsus and brought him to Antioch. There they spent a year teaching, praying, in fellowship and ministry with the believers in Antioch.

Agabus, a prophet from Jerusalem, came to share with the Antioch believers that a great famine was coming. These persons of Greek heritage and culture, newly converted to faith in Christ, immediately thought of the impact the famine would have on brothers and sisters in Christ back in Jerusalem. They were concerned for persons they had not met. They were concerned for persons who had serious doubts about Gentile Christians and would struggle to accept them. But that seemed to matter little. They had been made aware of the potential hunger and suffering of the believers in Jerusalem. So they determined to send a contribution to assist. They gave according to their means and put together funds to be carried by Paul and Barnabas as a love offering to be placed in the hands of the elders of the church in Jerusalem.

We encounter the Antioch church for a second time in Acts 13. They are enjoying the ministries of several prophets and teachers, Barnabas and Paul among them. But they are not so consumed with themselves that they cannot sense the Holy Spirit's urging them to share the gospel with others who have yet to hear. In obedience to the Spirit's urging, they commission Paul and Barnabas to leave them to preach Christ to the people of the Mediterranean region. They are the catalyst for the Paul and Barnabas's first missionary journey. Surely keeping Paul and Barnabas with them would have been in their best selfish interest. Believers would be added and discipled if these men continued to minister among them. But they were acutely aware that many needed to hear the gospel, and they were willing to support Paul and Barnabas in leaving them to preach to others.

The church at Antioch was capable of looking to the south and east to remember the Jerusalem community in a time of famine. They were able to look to the north and west to the population centers of Greece and Italy and share the apostles with persons who needed to know of Jesus. Somehow they were uniquely in tune with the Jesus' Great Commission, the will of God, the urging of the Spirit, and the needs of their world. Engaging in mission trumped selfishness. They shared their material and spiritual blessings freely with others in need.

It is a brief phrase inserted into the narratives of Antioch. But I believe it to be both important and intentional that in verse Acts 11:26 Luke writes, "It was in Antioch that the disciples were first called 'Christians.'" The Greek word *Christianos* takes the word *Christ* and attaches a borrowed Latin suffix which means "pertaining to, part of, or belonging to." At Antioch the word *Christian* emerges to describe these marvelous followers of Jesus as so completely attached to the risen Christ that they are called by others to be "miniature Christs"—persons who are full of Christ, totally connected to Christ, belonging to Christ. Believers in this church that can look beyond itself to respond to the needs of others are first called Christian. This church that is willing to share its resources to minister to the physical need of others in famine and to share its own ministers with those who have not heard the gospel is the first to be honored with the title *Christian.*

Perhaps we are too quick to call ourselves Christians. Perhaps *Christian* is a label that ought to be conferred by others rather than claimed by us. We use the term to describe someone who professes Christian belief. But many believed in Jesus and followed him before this term was first used. The first to be called Christians seemed quickly to comprehend that the Christ who calls us to believe opens our eyes to the needs of the world around us and expects us to minister to those needs. The global perspective of the church took root in Antioch. Then and there the believers were first called Christians.

Describing ministers who are missional leaders, Terry Hamrick writes: "Missional ministers possess a global perspective that informs their vision, nourishes their imagination, and pushes them into an ever-widening network of relationships. Increasingly, Christianity is a worldwide movement, and baptism into Christ joins us to a global community." He went on to say, "The global perspective that marks excellent ministry also contributes to a missional vision for the minister's work in her or his own congregation."

As with all of these sermons on the qualities of missional leaders, what Terry says about clergy I believe is just as true for every Christian. The Christian who lives with a global perspective will have a more vivid vision and imagination of what God is about in the world. This will in turn create passion and energy for being connected to and engaged in God's mission in the world. This global perspective will help us understand and respond to our own life situations. Nearsightedness and self-centeredness fail to equip us for meeting the challenges of our lives. But a Christ-focused view of the world and the part we are called to play in it never fails to bless our lives with the perspective and passion we need to lead amazing, fulfilling lives.

Becoming a Christ follower should correct the misconception that we are the center of our own universe. The world does not revolve around us. Self-absorption is the most traveled path into depression and discouragement. The necessary mind-changing of genuine repentance includes an exchange of being consumed with one's own personal issues for an authentic concern for others in the human family. Such a transformation brings the healing of Jesus to bear on some of the worst human attitudes and behaviors that result from caring only about ourselves and our friends and families, about our church and our community and our country, with little regard for the global community and the needs of the human family.

Ross Coggins died on August 1. I doubt his name rings a bell with you this morning. Let me tell you a little about him. He was born in 1927. He grew up in Texas during the Great Depression. Like many good Texas Baptists, he went to Baylor for his education. Called to ministry, he attended Southwestern Seminary in Fort Worth. He went to work for the Baptist General Convention of Texas as an associate in student ministry. A follower of Jesus, one worthy of the name Christian, can have a global perspective without being a world traveler. Ross Coggins had that global perspective; he was called to missions, and he served as a missionary to Indonesia. He was given the opportunity to lead USAID and worked passionately for relief to the poor throughout his life. Ross Coggins' eyes were opened to the world by his faith in Jesus, and he lived an extraordinary life because of it. You'll find Ross Coggins' name in your hymnal as he authored the lyrics of the wonderful hymn "Send Me, O Lord, Send Me."

God will not send every Christian traveling around the globe. But God will inspire every Christian to love the world that God has created and loved. And God will call every Christian to be keenly aware of and concerned for the world and to be open to the Spirit's call to heal and redeem and care for the world in Jesus' name. You may be called to pray, to give, to teach, to go, to serve, to send; but you will be saved from selfishness and called to live for a higher purpose. And when you take that salvation seriously and live life with a global perspective, you just might earn the title the believers at Antioch earned: someone may call you a true Christian.

I am grateful for a Baptist heritage and for members of this congregation who have helped me to have the global perspective needed to remain true to Jesus and to be a part of Great Commission faith. As a child, in Sunbeams and RAs, leaders introduced me to caring about all of God's people all over the globe. We learned about other cultures and the work of God's Spirit in those cultures to bring persons to faith in Jesus. I learned from committed WMU leaders about missionaries and their work among people of many nations and tribes. Those dear ladies did not have to travel the world to be concerned for it and engaged with it. They were faithful in doing mission work in their own community as they visited the sick and the elderly and cared for the needy even as they were supporting the work of God around the world.

I am so grateful to be a part of a congregation that, through its partnerships with other Baptists and Christians, is engaged in global mission. I am proud to see our youth made aware of the needs for clean water in Malawi and work to bring water to thirsty people. I am proud that youth and adults from our congregation travel to other parts of this country and the world to counter poverty and to work for peace and justice.

I am happy to be engaged in supporting a global missions team in CBF that seeks to be the presence of Christ among the most neglected people of the world. I am strengthened by the faith stories shared by our field personnel and honored to tell those stories in and with our children in Vacation Bible School.

My hope for every member of our congregation, young and old alike, is that our life of worship, service, and fellowship convicts us all to be less selfish, materialistic, and narrowly focused and inspires us all to be more globally aware, concerned, and generous.

We live in a culture that often promotes self-interest. Philosophers, authors, economists, and politicians abound that promote self-interest as a virtue. We worry about bank accounts, investment values, retirement portfolios, personal health, and personal fulfillment. How is this self-preoccupation working for us? About as well as selfishness has always worked. About as well as Jesus predicted the outcome for the self-absorbed.

And so, out of deep love and with amazing grace, God in Christ calls us to follow and to commit to caring for the uttermost parts of the earth. God calls us to be crucified to ourselves and to let Christ live in us. When Christ is living in us, we know it. We will be aware that we are a small part of the human family. We will be committed to the great mission of sharing God in Christ with all the family. And we will find that, healed of our deep illness of selfishness and given a new global awareness that takes seriously the needs of others, we have been saved to experience life that is new and fulfilling. And, maybe, with our newfound perspective and new way of living, someone may notice us and honor us by saying we remind them of Jesus. Yes, we are saved by grace. But we must live a Christlike life in order to be called Christian. May we live in just such a way.

SERMON DISCUSSION QUESTIONS
GLOBAL PERSPECTIVE

1. What impresses you about the New Testament narratives concerning the church at Antioch? How can our congregation become more like the church at Antioch?

2. Discuss the quote from Terry Hamrick: "Missional ministers possess a global perspective that informs their vision, nourishes their imagination, and pushes them into an ever-widening network of relationships. Increasingly Christianity is a worldwide movement, and baptism into Christ joins us to a global community."

3. What did you think of the idea that being called a Christian is not as much a name we take for ourselves because of what we believe but more a name we earn because our missional lifestyle indicates we truly belong to Jesus?

4. What important lessons about global perspective do we learn from the WMU era of missions education, prayer, support, and local involvement enhanced by global concern?

5. What important lessons do we learn from the current trend of short-term global mission engagement?

6. John Donne wrote, "No man is an island." How important is this idea of connectedness?

Strong Sense of Curiosity
Luke 11:1-13

This text from Luke's Gospel speaks to the importance of simplicity, perseverance, and trust. At the beginning of the passage, in response to the disciples' request to teach them how to pray, Jesus shares the simple model prayer. This is the shortened version, the one we Baptists are surprised to hear exists when we go to a Catholic service and hear something familiar and join in with gusto, only to be the only voice continuing with, "And deliver us from evil, for thine is the kingdom and the power and the glory, forever, Amen." We pray the prayer recorded in Matthew, a simple and direct prayer. But in Luke the prayer is even shorter and more to the point. When we pray, Jesus instructs us to acknowledge God's holiness, to ask for God's kingdom to come, to ask for daily bread, for forgiveness of sins, to acknowledge that we will in turn forgive others, and to request that we not be led into temptation. Keeping it simple is important.

At the end of the passage, Jesus emphasizes trust. Earthly parents, with all of our sin and imperfection, know how to give good gifts to our children. If we can trust ourselves, how much more should we trust God to give us what we need, to give us what is truly best for us?

The middle part of the passage, the part about persistence, will be our focus this morning. There Jesus encouraged the disciples to remain persistent in asking, seeking, and knocking. Late at night you may tell a friend and neighbor asking for bread to serve a surprise guest to come back in the morning. But, if the friend keeps knocking and asking for help, the reluctant neighbor will drag out of bed and give him what he asks, if for no other reason than to shut him up and get him off the doorstep hindering everyone's sleep.

So we are encouraged, we ask, and we keep on asking. Seek and keep on seeking. Knock and keep on knocking. Perhaps for no better reason than your aggravating persistence, you will receive your answer to your question, you will find what you have sought, and the door on which you knock will be opened to you.

Faith that is simple and direct, yet persistent and trusting, is encouraged by Jesus. He is encouraging us to be curious in our faith life enough to ask, to seek, and to knock. And, he is also encouraging us to be persistent. The answers are not always immediately forthcoming. Sometimes we search a long time before we find what we seek. Doors don't always open for us immediately. But, the promise is for those who remain persistent in their asking, seeking, and knocking.

In our continuing look at the qualities exhibited by missional Christian leaders this morning, we look at the fourth quality—a strong sense of curiosity. Terry Hamrick writes: "A strong sense of curiosity about the world, the church, and God's work with both is a quality found in missional leaders. Ministers who bring such a curiosity to their teaching and preaching exhibit a deep capacity for wonder and awe and a willingness to embrace mystery and uncertainty. This same curiosity compels a deeper commitment to a kind of study that searches for truth and meaning with a compelling persistence."

Albert Einstein said: "The important thing is not to stop questioning. Curiosity has its own reason for existing. One cannot help but be in awe when he contemplates the mysteries of eternity, of life, of the nameless structure of reality. I have no special talents. I am only passionately curious." Most of us recognize the value of a curious mind in asking the right questions and forming the right hypotheses that guide science. But most of us underestimate the value of curiosity in the spiritual and religious realms. God has called us to ask questions, to seek new things, to knock on closed doors, and to do these things with persistence.

Jesus taught that to enter the kingdom of God we must become like children. Perhaps one of the main reasons is that we need the curiosity of children to enter the kingdom. Every adult here this morning has had at least one moment when you were frustrated by the persistent curiosity of a child. Children are full of questions. They have the capacity for wonder. They are not easily put off. They are persistently curious. We need to become more like them in our faith.

My brother has served as the admissions chair for the medical school where he teaches. He is tough on those seeking admission, particularly in asking why they want to become a doctor. To those who have given more of a "beauty pageant" answer about wanting to help others, he encourages them to consider the career path of his brother, the minister, and to enroll in seminary instead of medical school. They are seldom amused.

In exasperation, some have asked, "What answer do you want? Why did you choose a career in medicine, teaching, and research?" He responds: "Since I was in ninth-grade biology, I have been fascinated with the human body and how it works. I have an insatiable curiosity to understand its systems, what happens when the body becomes ill or incapacitated, and how through biochemistry and pharmacology health can be preserved and illnesses treated."

God is looking for persons in the church, clergy and laity alike, to have just such a curiosity about all of life. It is a sad truth that too many Christians and congregations define their mission as defending a status quo and preserving tradition, and too few see our mission as questioning, seeking, and knocking that will lead to new and helpful understanding of the kingdom of God and how the kingdom may come on earth, even as it is in heaven.

Some of the best words or phrases for Christians are: "What if . . . ?" "I wonder what might happen if . . ." "Imagine . . ." "Do you think God might want us to . . ."

Much of Jesus' message focused on getting us to imagine a new world and a new way of living. His concept of the kingdom is all about imagining the world if it were to become the world God wants, the way things are prescribed in heaven. Listen to his teaching, and invariably it leads you to ask questions, to search for deeper meaning, to knock on the closed door. And inevitably the teaching of Jesus calls us to change. We ask, seek, and knock; and we find, discover, and open; and things change, from the status quo of a sinful world and all of its order to a bright new world where the first shall be last and the last shall be first. We imagine a world of loving our enemies, of talking to a Samaritan woman of bad reputation, of telling stories where the hero is of the despised race, of tax collectors gone straight, of an angry mob turned away from stoning an adulteress, of beggars in the bosom of Abraham, of prodigal sons welcomed home to a great feast, of lepers who are touched and made whole, of the blind who see, the lame who walk, and the insane who get unchained.

When we are curious about what God wants us to do, God can change the routine and the status quo. How could God's love change our community? How could life in our community mirror more of the kingdom of God? These are the right questions to ask. The persistent ones who ask, seek, and knock will find new discoveries of God's love in action and new ways to minister in Jesus' name. They will be the missional leaders of the church. How curious are you?

I commend the movie *The Help*. It is a compelling film, funny and heartwarming yet at the same time disturbing and troubling. It is about persons who are curious about why things are the way they are and who seek change that will make the world a better place. It is also a film about persons who left behind their wonder and curiosity in childhood and as adults cling to defending the world as it is and being closed to change, even when down deep they know that what they are defending is wrong.

Some people believe that faith in Christ can be used as a defense of the status quo. Their lives are lived righteously defending themselves as they are and the world as it is—all in the name of Jesus. They see no need to ask, seek, or knock. They believe they have all the answers, have found all the truth, and can be doorkeepers of what should be opened or closed.

That's not who I want to be. That's not the faith I want. I want to keep asking questions. I want to keep searching. I've got doors that need opening, so I stand and knock. Like the apostle said, "Now I see through the glass darkly," and, "Now I know in part, and I prophecy in part." Someday I will see everything clearly and know everything fully. But that day is not yet here. What I have now is an invitation from Jesus and an urging from the Spirit to keep asking, seeking, and knocking. I am to keep wondering about what God can do and about the kind of world God wants and about what part God wants me to play in it. I am called to journey in faith with you as a church family, to be curious about God's will for us, and to imagine the life we will share together and the newness we can bring to our community and world as we keep asking, keep seeking, and keep knocking.

SERMON DISCUSSION QUESTIONS
STRONG SENSE OF CURIOSITY

1. What images, ideas, or stories from the sermon caught your attention?

2. What things related to God, God's kingdom, the world, the spiritual life, and the mission of the church are you curious about?

3. Persistence in asking, seeking, and knocking is an emphasis of the passage and message. What hinders our persistence in asking, seeking and knocking?

4. Think of ways you have seen the curiosity of a Christian lead to action that advances the kingdom of God on earth?

5. Let's find where we are curious. Complete one of the statements below with what matters to you.

"I wonder what would happen if . . ."

"Imagine if . . ."

"What if we . . . ?"

Deep Love for the Church
Philippians 1:1-11

I have yet to plan many details of my funeral service. I hope that day is still a long way in the future. I have only planned one detail, and that is the song I want to be sung at the end of the service. It is my favorite hymn. I don't believe I have ever heard the song sung at a funeral before. It is the first hymn we sang this morning, "The Church's One Foundation."

Yes, at the end of that service, I want the people attending to sing about the church and Jesus, the foundation of the church. About the time they would roll my body out of the sanctuary for the last time, we should be about to the end of the first stanza, reminding everyone of God's grace as they sing, "From heaven he came and sought her to be his holy bride; with his own blood he bought her, and for her life he died." In the middle verse they will sing of the great communion of all the saints from every tribe and every nation. And, after my family is out of the room and the congregation sings to the end of the hymn, the final words of that day will be, "Till with the vision glorious, her longing eyes are blest, and the great church victorious shall be the church at rest." Indeed, on that day I will have seen Christ face-to-face, and I will be at rest. It makes little difference what else may be said or sung that day, but I want people to celebrate that I lived my life as part of the church, the body and bride of Christ.

This morning we are focusing on the fifth of five qualities exhibited by missional leaders—deep love for the church. Terry Hamrick writes: "Missional ministers exhibit a deep love for the church. They understand the central role of the church in the mission of God. This is not a love that denies the struggles present in human life but a love rooted both in the love of Christ and in an ongoing awareness of the presence of the risen Christ in the church."

Sadly, we live in a time when it is fairly popular to direct frustration and criticism at the church. The church is decried as an institution undeserving of loyalty in a postmodern society. Some say one of the marks of the present age is a suspicion of institutions, and suspicion runs high when it comes to the church. The criticism of the church is not just from persons outside the church; the critique often comes from those who are all about loving and following Jesus but have little regard for the church and congregational life. I know I swim upstream against this swift and strong current of antichurch talk and feeling. I would not for a minute overlook or deny the church's shortcomings in how we treat one another, how we treat persons outside the church, and the poor job we do of passionately engaging in mission because we are more interested in having our own needs met. But I still love the imperfect church. I believe loving the church is compatible with the missional lifestyle of a committed follower of Jesus. In fact, I believe loving the church enhances one's commitment to God and to the mission of God in the world.

I am able to love the church for all the reasons the apostle Paul loved the church. He expresses deep love and affection for the church at Philippi. Years before he wrote this letter, Paul had traveled there and preached the gospel. Lydia and all of her household, the jailer and his household were some of the first believers who came to faith on Paul's visit to Philippi. Now Paul is writing to encourage all of the believers there. Let's look at Paul's deep love and affection for them.

"I thank my God every time I remember you" (v. 3). Paul remembers the people of God and is grateful for each remembrance. When he prays for them, he prays with joy. He is confident in their continued growth in the faith. God has begun a good work in them, but God is not yet finished. Paul longs to be with them. He is unashamed to express his affection for them. He appreciates that they are co-laborers with him, that they are partners with his ministry. And so he is positive about their future. Their love will abound even more. Their knowledge and discernment will grow even more. They will find their way to be excellent and to do excellent things. They will bring praise and glory to God.

Like Paul, I thank God for my memories and thoughts of the people of the church. I remember the church of my childhood. I remember teachers from my childhood who loved and nurtured me. I remember my baptism and the way adults in the church affirmed me in making the decision to follow Christ. I remember those who were instrumental in my coming to faith in Jesus.

I thank God for remembrances of the church of my later youth and college years and the church of my ordination. I remember college Bible studies in leaders' homes, people who had a passion for seeing college-age students grow in their relationship with God. I remember those who trusted me to teach their children and youth, who helped me discover the joy of ministry as I began to sense God's calling.

All of you are part of my joyful memories and ongoing experiences. I am the minister I am today because of the many ways I have been shaped by people in this congregation. Many of you have loved me and prayed for me. I can never repay you. I can just thank my God with every remembrance.

The church is not buildings, budgets, and institutions. It is a group of real people, a family of faith, brothers and sisters in Christ. To engage in the fellowship of the church is amazing and wonderful. I have had deep experiences of love and grace that words cannot adequately describe.

To a generation skeptical of the church's relevance and doubtful of its future, hear a word of caution. The church is the bride of Christ. I don't know of any groom who appreciates criticism of his bride. I count Jesus in that number. Imperfect? Yes. Enduring periods of decline and struggle? Yes. Sometimes off the mark? Yes. But by God's grace the church will make it through the storms.

I want the mission of God to advance on earth. I want to be a part of that mission. Some would argue that they can do that without the church, maybe even better without the church. I disagree.

I need the worship and fellowship of the church. And my own zeal and passion for the mission of God will be enhanced, not hindered, by the church. I am like Mattie Rigsbee in Clyde Edgerton's novel, *Walking Across Egypt*. The church is good for us. It will put a robustness in our step and color in our cheeks. It is good to be around the young and the old, people being kind to one another, caring for one another, all because of a shared faith in Jesus.

Why do I believe a deep love for the church is a quality needed in a missional leader? I guess I can say it best with this last story. I was walking to my car in the parking lot to drive to Raleigh to visit hospitals. A man approached me, staggering a bit. He said as he neared, "You're the preacher here. I just want to talk to you for a minute." His eyes were glazed, and he struggled to focus. I did not know what he wanted to say, but I figured he would probably ask for money.

Instead the man said, "I just need to thank you and your church. You helped my mama this winter. She has been sick, and she was out of heating oil. You helped her fill her prescription, and you filled up her tank with heating oil." He choked back tears and said, "When this old sorry son could not help his mama, your church did. I want to thank you." He gave me a quick hug and went on his way. In that moment I knew that the fellowship of the church and the mission of God are inseparable.

I am glad my life's work has been in the church. And I am grateful that while you earn your living elsewhere, so many of you have loved the church, and it too is your life's work. Let's keep on keeping on, loving the church; and let's try our best to be the hands and feet of Jesus whenever we can.

When Nathan Parrish was a student at Wake Forest he heard Warren Kerr preach a sermon on the church. Warren ran the church down pretty good in his invitation. He spoke of all of the faults and shortcomings of the church. Warren concluded, "But you might as well join up. For all of its flaws and failures, the church of Jesus Christ is still the best thing this old world has going for it. You will be joining a messed-up, flawed group of folks, and you will only add to their mess. But join up and join in, and your life will never be the same. You will be glad you did. And what's more, God will be glad you did." I can't improve on that invitation.

SERMON DISCUSSION QUESTIONS
DEEP LOVE FOR THE CHURCH

1. Why do you believe confidence in the church has been eroded? What can the church do to restore confidence in it?

2. What is seriously missing from the life of a believer in Christ who tries to follow Jesus apart from participation in the church?

3. If our church were suddenly to exist no longer, what would you miss? What do you think other members of the congregation of varying ages would miss? What would our community miss? What would the world miss?

4. Discuss the assertion of the sermon that deep love for the church is an important quality found in missional leaders. Do you believe this to be true?

5. How can a congregation enhance the reputation of the church in its community?

6. We have now looked at the five qualities of missional leaders — resurrection confidence, robust spirituality, global perspective, a deep sense of curiosity, and strong love for the church. Which ones do you see as most important? How do you see these qualities reflected in the lives of those who are missional leaders in our congregation? How can we develop these qualities in one another? Can you think of other qualities not included in our list?

www.ingramcontent.com/pod-product-compliance
Lightning Source LLC
Chambersburg PA
CBHW050828160426
43192CB00010B/1940